NEB

THE **ULTIMATE WOODSHOP**
JIG BOOK

R.J. DECRISTOFORO

PHOTOS AND DRAWINGS BY THE AUTHOR

POPULAR WOODWORKING BOOKS
CINCINNATI, OHIO

METRIC CONVERSION CHART

TO CONVERT	TO	MULTIPLY BY
Inches	Centimeters	2.54
Centimeters	Inches	0.4

The Ultimate Woodshop Jig Book. Copyright © 1999 by R.J. DeCristoforo. Printed and bound in the United States of America. All rights reserved. No part of this book may be reproduced in any form or by any electronic or mechanical means including information storage and retrieval systems without permission in writing from the publisher, except by a reviewer, who may quote brief passages in a review. Published by Popular Woodworking Books, an imprint of F&W Publications, Inc., 1507 Dana Avenue, Cincinnati, Ohio 45207. (800) 289-0963. First edition.

Other fine Popular Woodworking Books are available from your local bookstore or direct from the publisher.

03 02   5 4 3

Library of Congress Cataloging-in-Publication Data

DeCristoforo, R.J.
     The ultimate woodshop jig book / by R.J. DeCristoforo : photos and drawings by the author.
          p.   cm.
     Includes index.
     ISBN 1-55870-491-4 (pb : alk. paper)
     1. Woodworking machinery. 2. Jigs and fixtures. I. Title.
TS850.D35   1999
684'.083—dc21   98-40932
                                                                      CIP

Editor: R. Adam Blake
Content editor: Bruce Stoker
Production editor: Marilyn Daiker
Production coordinator: Kristen Heller
Interior and cover designer: Mary Barnes Clark

For my friend & wife Mary
and
to Daniel, David and Ronald.

ABOUT THE AUTHOR

By age eighteen, R.J. "Cris" DeCristoforo knew that his career had to be in the field of writing. He took on a part-time job for "bread and butter" money and was encouraged by placement of poetry and the sale of fiction and articles to general publications. It wasn't until he realized he could combine his writing and interest in woodworking that his career really took off. A first sale of a project to *Popular Science Magazine* is what did it. In a six-by-ten-foot basement workshop that was equipped with an assortment of hand tools, an electric drill and the motor he salvaged from an old coffee grinder, he was able to produce how-to stories for every magazine in the country that welcomed that type of material. His output included articles ranging from leathercraft to metal etching in addition to his favorite subject, woodworking.

Today, some several thousand articles and more than forty books later, to the readers of magazines and books in the home workshop field, the name R.J. DeCristoforo is associated with originality and daring in the creative use of tools. His philosophy is "learn to do it the traditional way and then discover a better, safer, faster, more convenient method of accomplishing the chore."

Cris now lives with friend/wife Mary in Los Altos Hills, California, in a ranch-style house they built almost from scratch with the aid of three sons. Editors who visit him are surprised at his workshop. "It's just an oversize two-car garage with tools in it," he says and adds, "It's what you do with the tools that counts, not how you house them."

TABLE OF CONTENTS

INTRODUCTION

If you work with tools you will inevitably be faced with a chore that can be accomplished more accurately, faster or safer, by using a jig. Jigs can help you clone any number of project components, make more feasible a particular application that's difficult to accomplish by textbook means, minimize if not eliminate the bugaboo of human error. You won't find plans for jigs in owner's manuals and few are offered commercially, and when available, can tax the woodworking budget.

A jig is an accessory that's custom made. It might be a quick assembly to solve a one-time chore but, more often, it becomes as permanently useful as the tool on which it was designed to be used. Many times, the project enables you to extend the applications of a tool beyond its basic functions. Simple or complex, jigs are a bridge to more competent woodworking.

It's been said that only amateurs need the assurance and extra hands that jigs provide. Don't believe it! I've yet to visit a commercial woodworking establishment or the home shop of an "expert" amateur that didn't host a plenitude of helpmates. Another negative thought is that only the pros have the expertise to make jigs. I don't know what prompted such a false theory. It's likely that professionals have the edge when *inventing* an accessory since they are more involved in the world of woodworking, but duplicating an idea that's been shop tested and is presented with clear drawings and other illustrations is within the scope of anyone.

Jigs work in various ways. A unit like a *Tenoning Jig* secures and positions a workpiece so it can be moved accurately past a saw blade while keeping hands out of the danger zone. A *Mitering Jig* for a table saw eliminates the errors that can occur when using the miter gauge to move the work; slight errors usually, but they add up to frustration at assembly time when faced with a frame that is "out of square."

Some concepts reverse the usual way a tool is used. The *Master Jig for a Portable Router* establishes the tool in a fixed position so it's used as a stationary machine. It is often more convenient to move the work without the worry of controlling the tool.

Often, a lot of changes occur between the drawing board (or computer monitor) and final acceptance of the idea. I visualized an oversize table for a band saw—certainly a practical add-on—but once made and tested, it followed naturally that there could be more here than extra support surface. By including provisions for a fence and miter gauge, incorporating a slide for circular sawing, adding attachments for sawing rounds and halving cyclinders, and more, the original idea evolved as the *Master Jig for a Band Saw*.

Some jigs are designed out of downright necessity. How do you flute a table or chair leg without providing for holding the work in correct position and guiding a router? How can you guide a router for circular cuts and how can you ensure a perfect sanded edge when a circular piece is sawed on a band saw or other tool? These and similar woodworking problems are solved with jigs.

Jigs are getting a lot of attention these days, to the point of being commercialized. Many of the plans being offered suggest, or make it necessary to send away for a kit that often includes special extrusions and fancy hardware, sometimes even the wood that is needed. It's a way to go, but it's costly and involves a wait period before the project can be started. Much of the fun of jig making is being able to start *now*, and with materials readily available from local lumber yards and hardware stores. If you have done some woodworking it's likely that what you need to make a particular jig is already in the shop.

Improvising is also part of the scene. You can make a wing bolt by peening a wing nut on the end of a length of threaded rod. A hold-down can be a specially shaped piece of hardwood. You can make a lock screw by bending a machine bolt into an L-shape after removing its head. Threaded inserts that are available in many sizes and in coarse or fine threads are great for attaching components.

I enjoy making jigs and have designed quite a few of them, but it's not an obsession. In the course of my woodworking I often encounter a chore that makes me pause and think. Is there a better, safer, faster way to do this? And a jig is born. Often, an idea is prompted by a neighborhood woodworker or a reader asking advice about a particular chore. I admit, too, to occasionally being inspired by a published project and thinking it could be better or expanded.

In the final analysis, a jig must be a practical accessory, fun and reasonably easy to produce. But it must be carefully made. Jig making is one activity where it's valid to take ten minutes to do a five-minute job. If you consider that a jig can be a lifetime tool, you'll agree that making it right is the only way to go.

And, while making it right, be aware, as always, of your own well being. Obey all the safety rules and remember my oft-repeated phrases—*"measure twice, cut once"* and *"think twice before cutting."*

Miter Gauge Extension

With the stop locked in an elevated position, the extension can provide good support for crosscutting long pieces of work. Mark a cut line on the work so it can be lined up with the kerf in the fence when the cut is required at a particular point.

A miter gauge extension is a primary project for any table saw. The most elementary design is simply a straight piece of wood that is much longer and as high, or a bit higher, than the head of the miter gauge. It serves a purpose, but our concept includes a sliding stop and an add-on attachment for sawing the cheek cuts required for tenons. As such, it might be called a "fence" that positions work at right angles to the saw blade.

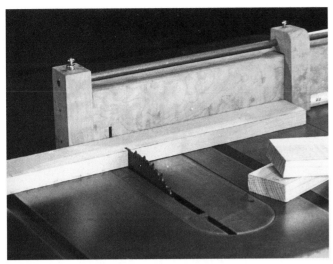

The stop is locked at a particular point to gauge the length of any number of similar pieces. Cut pieces are shown only for the sake of the photo. Don't let pieces accumulate near the danger zone. Set blade projection only enough to get through the work.

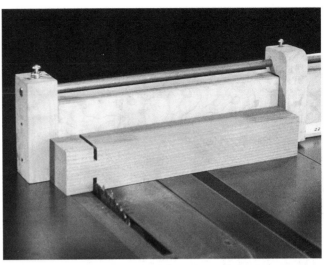

Shoulder cuts for tenons are made in normal crosscut position. The distance from the end of the work to the blade equals the length of the tenon. The projection of the blade determines the tenon's thickness.

The support for tenoning is locked in place to suit the thickness of the wood less the material that will be sawed off. The distance setting is from the support to the *facing* side of the saw blade.

Always position the work when making cheek cuts so the waste falls free of the saw blade. Use the hold-in in the threaded insert that's most suitable in relation to the projection of the saw blade. Don't set it *lower* than the height of the blade.

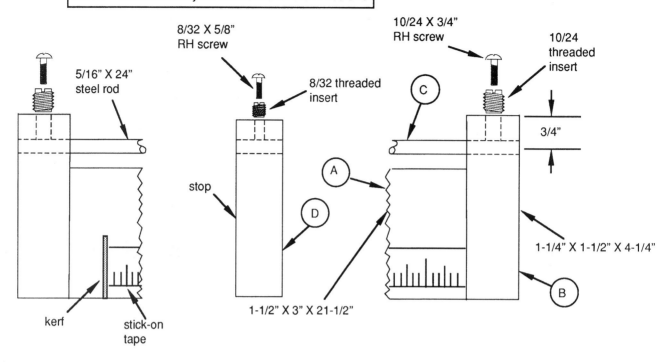

NOTE -- set screws may be substituted for the RH screws

5/16" X 24" steel rod

8/32 X 5/8" RH screw

8/32 threaded insert

stop

10/24 X 3/4" RH screw

10/24 threaded insert

3/4"

C

A

D

1-1/4" X 1-1/2" X 4-1/4"

B

1-1/2" X 3" X 21-1/2"

kerf

stick-on tape

MATERIALS LIST				
MITER GAUGE EXTENSION				
QTY.	KEY	NAME	SIZE (IN INCHES)	MATERIAL
1	A	Fence	1½ × 3 × 21½	Hardwood
2	B	End	1¼ × 1½ × 4¼	Hardwood
1	C	Rod	5⁄16 × 24	Steel Rod
1	D	Stop	1⅛ × 1¾ × 4	Hardwood
Tenoning Accessory				
QTY.	KEY	NAME	SIZE (IN INCHES)	MATERIAL
1	E	Support	1½ × 4 × 8	Hardwood
1	F	Holder	¾ × 3 × 3¼	Hardwood
1	G	Disc	1 × ⅜	Hardwood (or Wheel)

24" Length Stick-On Measuring Tape   10/24 Threaded Insert (4)

⅜" × 5" Threaded Rod with Wing Nut (1)   10/24 × ¾" Round Head Screw (2)

⅜" Threaded Insert (2)   8/32 × ⅝" Round Head Screw (1)

8/32 Threaded Insert (2)   8/32 × ¾" Round Head Screw (1)

STEP 1: MAKE THE FENCE

Start by preparing a piece of hardwood 1½″×3″×21½″. Then cut the ends (B) to size and carefully mark the locations of the holes; for the steel rod, centered and ¾″ O.C. from top of (B); and for the threaded insert, centered on top of (B). Form the holes on a drill press to be sure they will be square to surfaces. Install the inserts and after coating the mating surfaces of the fence and ends with glue, keep them together with a bar clamp until the glue sets. It's a good idea to have the steel bar in place during the gluing process to ensure alignment of the parts.

STEP 2: ATTACH FENCE TO MITER GAUGE

Clamp the fence to the miter gauge so its end extends to the right of the saw blade about 3″. Drill through the holes in the miter gauge to spot the locations of the threaded inserts. Then, remove the fence, enlarge the holes and install the inserts. The fence could be attached with ordinary wood screws, but using inserts will add to the accuracy of the jig.

With the fence in place, use a triangle or square to be sure the angle between the fence and the saw blade is 90°. Set the blade about a 1½″ projection and move the unit forward to

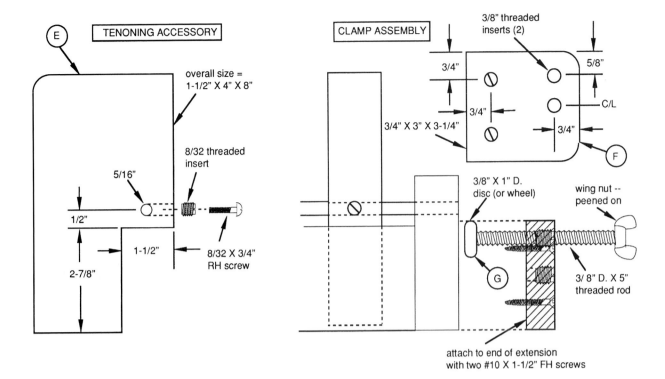

TENONING ACCESSORY

E

overall size = 1-1/2" X 4" X 8"

8/32 threaded insert

5/16"

1/2"

1-1/2"

8/32 X 3/4" RH screw

2-7/8"

CLAMP ASSEMBLY

3/8" threaded inserts (2)

3/4"

5/8"

3/4"

C/L

3/4" X 3 X 3-1/4"

3/4"

F

3/8" X 1" D. disc (or wheel)

wing nut -- peened on

G

3/8" D. X 5" threaded rod

attach to end of extension with two #10 X 1-1/2" FH screws

---

form a kerf through the fence.

Attach a length of self-stick measuring tape to the fence, making sure that its starting point is exactly on the left side of the kerf.

STEP 3: MAKE THE STOP

Cut the part (D on page 10) to overall size and drill the holes required for the steel bar and the threaded insert. Install the insert and then rough-cut the stop to the shape shown in the diagram at right. It's best to "fine-tune" the stop by hand to be sure it slides smoothly on the steel bar and can pivot without interference.

STEP 4: MAKE THE TENONING ACCESSORY

Cut the support (E) to overall size and after installing the threaded insert, saw out the notch at its bottom, inside corner. The support doesn't tilt, but like the stop, it should move smoothly on the bar without interference from the fence.

Start the clamp assembly by shaping the holder (F) and installing the

stop -- full size (1/4" squares)

two ⅜" threaded inserts. Place the holder against the end of the fence and drill for the screws that will secure the component. No glue is used

here since the accessory is added only when needed. The pad on the end of the threaded rod can be a disc formed with a hole saw, or a toy wheel that might be on hand. It can even be a rubber bumper.

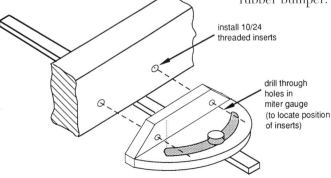

install 10/24 threaded inserts

drill through holes in miter gauge (to locate position of inserts)

Compound Angle Jig

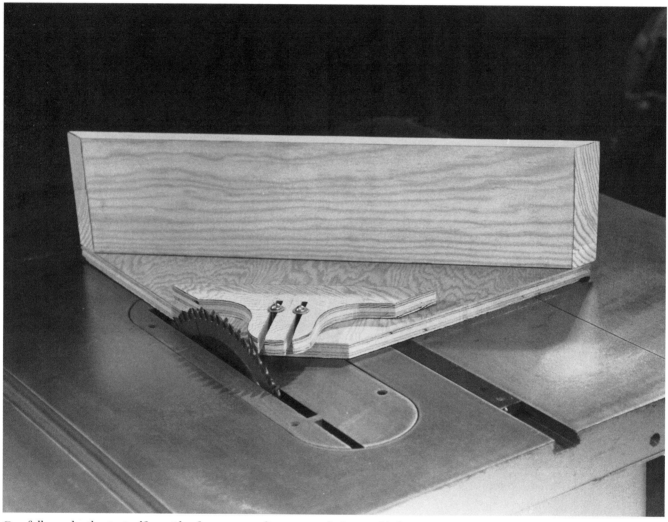

Carefully made, the jig itself provides for accurate alignment with the saw blade.

A simple miter cut can be a frustrating chore simply because of the precise saw cuts that are needed. A slight error, even less than one degree, is multiplied by eight when making a square or rectangular frame, for example, and the consequence is evident at assembly time. The conventional cutting method for a compound angle requires a blade tilt plus a miter-gauge setting. The settings must mesh perfectly to provide the required slope angle to the sides and a 90° turn at the corners.

There are charts that provide the settings for particular angles but it's a cut-and-try method. Rarely can you produce an accurate joint just by using the machine's scale readings to make adjustments. The chore is further complicated by the fact that the two settings interact. If you eliminate one setting—the blade tilt—you reduce the possibility of human error by half.

That's the purpose of the compound angle jig. You set the work-slope with a T-bevel or by eye. In some cases—crown and cove molding—the slope is established by the material.

Incidentally, the slope-angle is not

always critical so long as it's visually pleasing. Only a persnickety critic would judge a project like a picture frame or planter on the basis of whether the slope angle should have been a few degrees more or less.

STEP 1: MAKE THE BASE AND FENCE

Cut the fence (A) and the base (B) to the sizes shown in the materials list. Then shape each end of both parts to a 45° angle. Do this by carefully marking the cut-lines and sawing a bit outside the lines. Finish exactly to the lines by working on a disc or belt sander.

Drill the holes for the threaded inserts and, after installing them, join the base to the fence with glue and no. 8 × 1½" flathead screws.

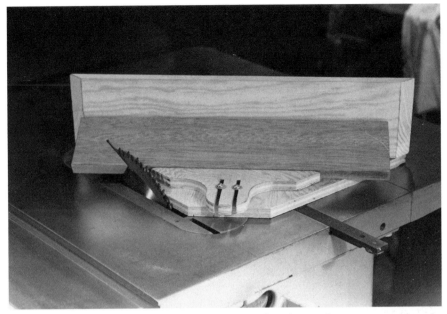

The jig is used as if making a simple 45° miter cut, but the result is a compound angle. This occurs regardless of the slope angle of the work.

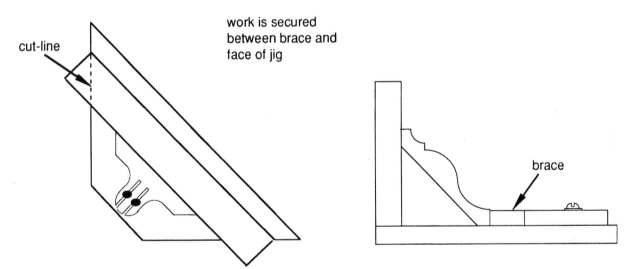

cut-line

work is secured between brace and face of jig

brace

The position of the brace sets the slope angle of the work. Some materials, like cove and crown moldings, establish their own slope angle.

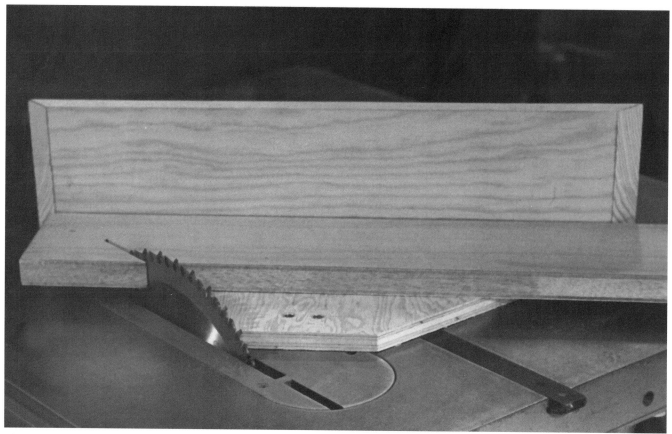

The jig, with the brace removed, is usable for simple miter cuts.

MATERIALS LIST				
COMPOUND ANGLE JIG				
QTY.	KEY	NAME	SIZE (IN INCHES)	MATERIAL
1	A	Fence	¾ × 4 × 18	Optional
1	B	Base	½ × 7 × 18	Plywood
1	C	Brace	½ × 4⅛ × 8½	Plywood
10/24 Threaded Insert (6)			No. 8 × 1½″ Flathead Screw (4)	
10/24 × 1″ Round Head Screw with Washer (2)			10/24 × 1¼″ Round Head Screw (2)	

STEP 2: MAKE THE BRACE

Cut the part (C) to overall size and then mark the location of the slots. Form the slots by drilling ³⁄₁₆″ end-holes and then sawing out the waste. Now, finish forming the brace to the shape shown in the drawing.

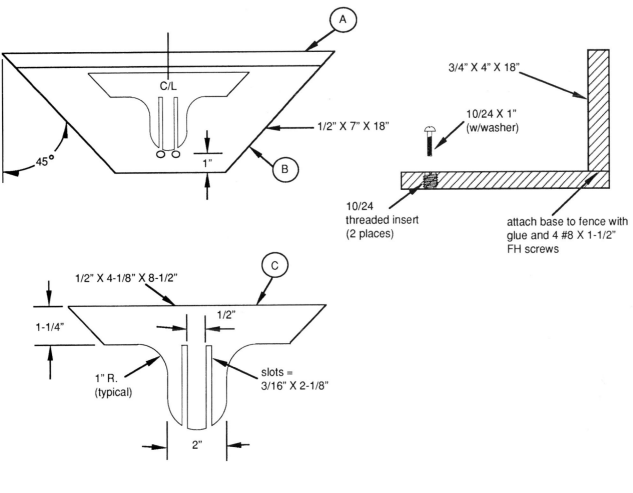

A

C/L

1/2" X 7" X 18"

B

45°

1"

3/4" X 4" X 18"

10/24 X 1"
(w/washer)

10/24
threaded insert
(2 places)

attach base to fence with
glue and 4 #8 X 1-1/2"
FH screws

C

1/2" X 4-1/8" X 8-1/2"

1/2"

1-1/4"

1" R.
(typical)

slots =
3/16" X 2-1/8"

2"

TWO SETS OF MOUNTING
HOLES ARE NEEDED FOR
THE COMPOUND ANGLE JIG

install 10/24
threaded inserts
(4 places)

drill through
holes in
miter gauge
(to locate position
of inserts)

STEP 3: ATTACH THE JIG TO THE MITER GAUGE

Set the miter gauge at 45° and place it in the right-hand table slot. Clamp the jig to the miter gauge so its left, 45° edge is flush against the saw blade. Adjust the miter gauge if necessary. Drill through the holes in the miter gauge to mark the locations of the first pair of threaded inserts. Repeat the procedure with the miter gauge placed in the left-hand table slot. Installing the four inserts completes construction of the jig.

A Jig for the Fingerlap Joint

The fingerlap jig is designed as an independent tool. It's critical that the groove formed by the dadoing tool matches the width of the joint's fingers. Make the depth of the cut a fraction more than needed so the fingers can be sanded flush after assembly.

The fingerlap joint, like the dovetail, is often found on classic furniture, exposed at times because of its appearance, and used in hidden areas because of its strength. It doesn't have a locking feature like the dovetail, but its structural appeal lies in the intertwining fingers and the considerable amount of glue area they provide.

It's often stated that the cut-width should be equal to the stock's thickness. It's a "rule" to be broken. My preference is for a finger-width of ¼″ on any material up to ¾″-thick. You may agree that the thought leads to a more attractive connection. It certainly provides greater strength (see the top of page 17).

Some jigs are quite elaborate and are attached to the miter gauge. Since the chore simply involves cutting a series of notches of equal width and depth, why complicate it? The jig I use, like the feathering jig, is an independent unit with double miter gauge bars so firm support is provided on both sides of the cutter.

MAKING THE JIG

STEP 1: BARS AND BRACE

Make a subassembly of the bars (B) and brace (C). Attach the bars to the braces with glue and 4d finishing nails. Drill pilot holes through the bars before driving the nails.

STEP 2: MAKE THE FACE

Cut the face (A) to overall size. Put the subassemblies on the table and position the face so you can mark the location of the dado-cuts. Form the dadoes and then attach the face to the braces with no. $8 \times 1\frac{1}{2}''$ flathead screws. Do not use glue at this point.

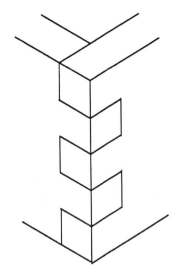

3/4" fingers on
3/4" stock

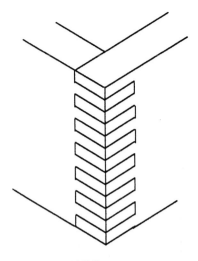

1/4" fingers on
3/4" stock

The work is positioned by placing the last groove that was cut over the guide strip. Hold the workpieces firmly against the face of the jig.

MATERIALS LIST				
FINGERLAP JIG				
QTY.	KEY	NAME	SIZE (IN INCHES)	MATERIAL
1	A	Face	$\frac{3}{4} \times 5 \times 17\frac{1}{2}$	Optional
2	B	Bar	$\frac{3}{8} \times \frac{3}{4} \times 14$	Hardwood
2	C	Brace	$\frac{3}{4} \times 4 \times 5$	Optional
1	D	Backup	$\frac{3}{4} \times 1\frac{1}{2} \times 3\frac{1}{2}$	Hardwood
1	E	Guide/Spacer	(Make To Suit)	Hardwood
No. $8 \times 1\frac{1}{2}''$ Flathead Screw (4)				

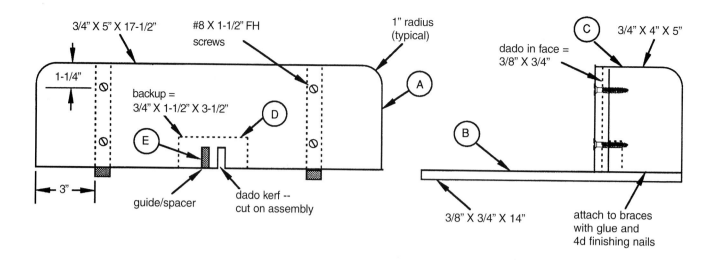

3/4" X 5" X 17-1/2"

#8 X 1-1/2" FH
screws

1" radius
(typical)

1-1/4"

backup =
3/4" X 1-1/2" X 3-1/2"

(A)

(D)

(E)

3"

guide/spacer

dado kerf --
cut on assembly

(C) 3/4" X 4" X 5"

dado in face =
3/8" X 3/4"

(B)

3/8" X 3/4" X 14"

attach to braces
with glue and
4d finishing nails

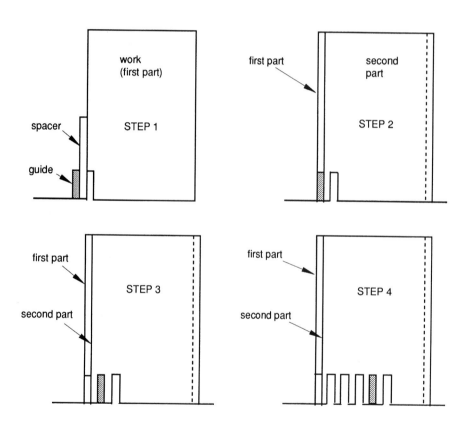

work
(first part)

STEP 1

spacer

guide

first part

second
part

STEP 2

first part

STEP 3

second part

first part

STEP 4

second part

STEP 3: MAKE THE FIRST NOTCH

Set up a dadoing tool to cut ¼"-wide, using shims with a dado assembly if necessary, and adjusting a variable dado to be sure the cut-width is correct. Make test cuts in scrap stock before committing the tool to use.

Adjust the projection of the cutter so it equals the width of the stock plus a bit more. This is so the fingers can be sanded flush after assembly. Place the jig in position and move it forward to cut the first notch in the face.

STEP 4: THE SECOND NOTCH

Remove the face from the jig and carefully mark the location of the second notch to the right of the first one. Cut this notch using the miter gauge after assuring that the angle between the gauge and the cutter is 90°.

Attach the backup (D) to the face with glue and then put the face into position against the braces, this time using glue in addition to the screws.

FINAL STEP: MAKE THE GUIDE/SPACER

Use hardwood for the guide/spacer (E), sizing a 4" or 5" strip so its thickness and width matches the notches in the jig. Cut off about 2″ of the strip and glue it in the right-hand notch. The remainder of the strip will be used as a spacer when the jig is put to use.

USING THE JIG

Before you start cutting, be aware that the width of the sides of the project must be sized in increments of the finger-width. Since the jig is designed for ¼″ cuts, the sides must be, say, 4″ or 4¼″, or 6″ or 6¼″, and so on. Otherwise, you'll have partial fingers at one end of the work.

Start by placing the spacer strip against the guide and the first part of the work against the strip. Firmly hold spacer and work, and advance the jig to make the first cut, actually a notch. Remove the spacer and place the first part so the notch is over the guide. Then place the mating part of the joint so it butts against the guide, and make a second cut. The work is positioned for the following cuts by placing the last groove that was cut over the guide.

VARIATIONS

You can change the appearance of the fingerlap joint by chamfering the corner or rounding it. "Dress" the fingers suitably and you can produce a swivel joint. Drill the hole for the pin before modifying the fingers.

Another use for the fingerlap jig, or a similar one, is making the cuts for dentil molding. Make the cuts in a thick piece of stock and then slice it into strips of suitable thickness.

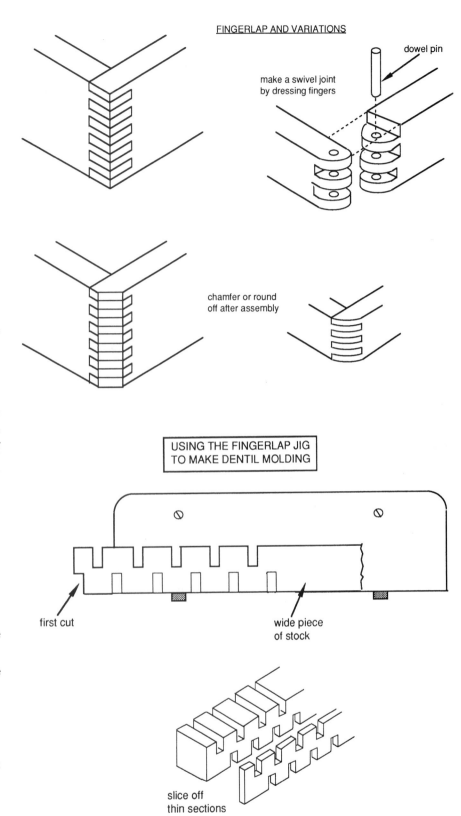

FINGERLAP AND VARIATIONS

make a swivel joint by dressing fingers

dowel pin

chamfer or round off after assembly

USING THE FINGERLAP JIG TO MAKE DENTIL MOLDING

first cut

wide piece of stock

slice off thin sections

Feathering Jig

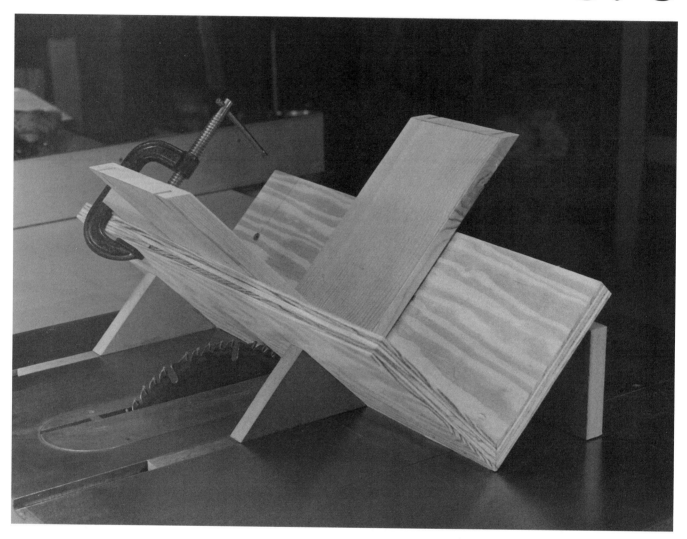

Feathers, sometimes called "keys," are triangular splines that serve several purposes. They strengthen miter joints, make it easier to do assembly work and, when made of a contrasting material, supply a detail that adds to the appearance of the project. Cutting the necessary grooves, or "keyways," individually can be time-consuming and leads to human error. Accuracy is automatic when using the feathering jig since mating cuts are made simultaneously. This type of project is often designed for use with a miter gauge. The one I use is guided by its own "miter gauge bars," so it's an independent tool, always ready for use.

MATERIALS LIST				
FEATHERING JIG				
QTY.	KEY	NAME	SIZE (IN INCHES)	MATERIAL
2	A	Guide	$\frac{3}{8} \times \frac{3}{4} \times 15$	Hardwood
2	B	Brace	$\frac{3}{4} \times 3 \times 4$	Optional
1	C	Fence	$\frac{3}{4} \times 4 \times 20$	Optional
2	D	Inner Brace	$\frac{3}{4} \times \times 4 \times 4\frac{1}{4}$	Optional
4	E	Outer Brace	$\frac{3}{4} \times 4 \times 4$	Optional
2	F	Trough	$\frac{3}{4} \times 6 \times 20$	Optional
No. $6 \times 1''$ Flathead Screw (12)			No. $8 \times 1\frac{1}{2}$ Flathead Screw (8)	

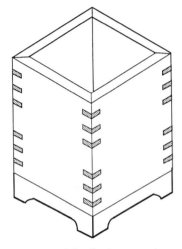

Spacing of the feathers is arbitrary. Use a contrasting material or one that blends with the project.

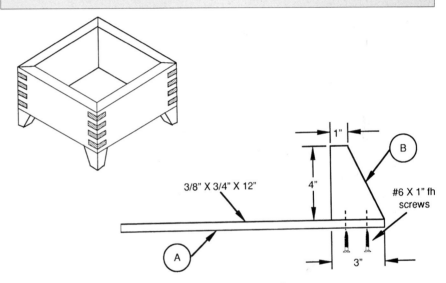

Start the project by attaching the brace (B) to the guide bar. Two assemblies are needed.

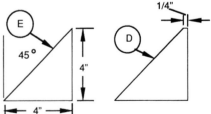

Locate the position of the back-to-back dadoes by having the subassemblies in place on the saw.

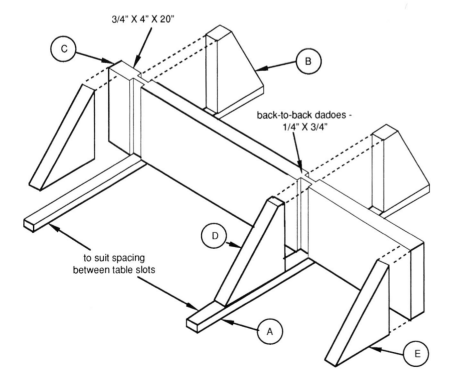

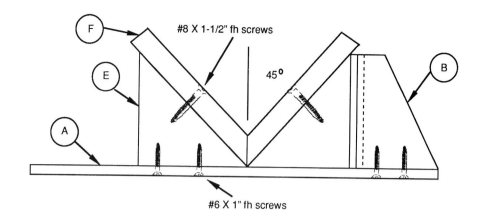

#8 X 1-1/2" fh screws

45°

F

E

A

B

#6 X 1" fh screws

FRONT VIEW

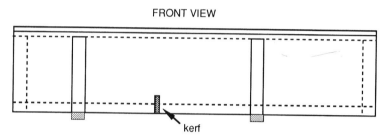

kerf

The two pieces for the trough are mitered so the angle between them is 90°.

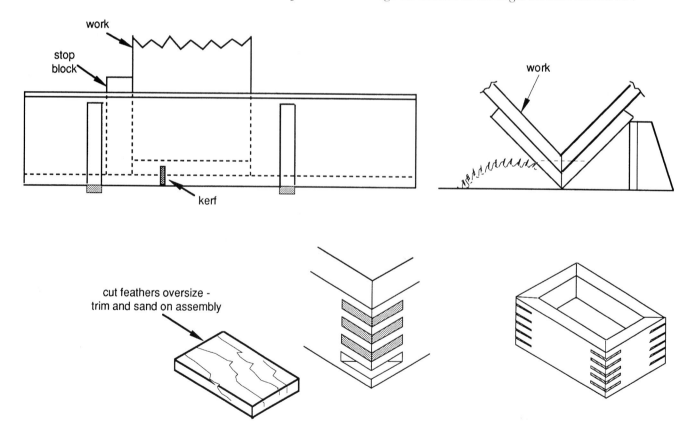

work

stop block

kerf

work

cut feathers oversize - trim and sand on assembly

Clamp a strip of wood to the jig as a stop to gauge the position of the work.

MAKING THE JIG

STEP 1: GUIDES AND BRACE

Make a subassembly of parts (A) and (B). Size the guides so they will slide smoothly in the table saw slots. Attach a brace at the end of each guide with glue and no. 6 × 1″ flathead screws. Drill adequate holes for the screws so they can be installed without spreading the guides.

STEP 2: ADD THE FENCE AND FOUR BRACES

Cut the fence to size and use a dadoing tool to form the back-to-back dadoes. Have the subassemblies in place so you can determine the spacing for the cuts. Install the fence by gluing it to the braces of the subassembly.

Next, form the inner braces (D) and the outer braces (E). Note that the inner braces are ¼″ wider since they fit in the dadoes that are in the fence. Glue them to the fence and the guides and then add the two no. 6 × 1″ flathead screws that are installed through the bottom of the guides. Attach the outer braces with glue and, optionally, add a couple of 4d finishing nails.

STEP 3: ADD THE TROUGH

Cut the parts for the trough to overall size and then saw one edge of each to 45°. The angle between the bearing surfaces of the two parts after they are joined must be 90°.

Use glue and no. 8 × 1½″ flathead screws to attach one part of the trough to the braces that are already

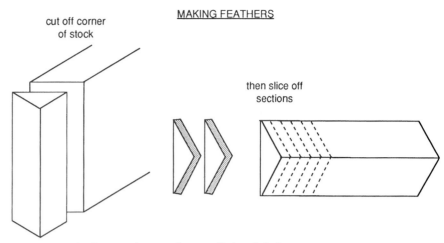

cut off corner of stock

<u>MAKING FEATHERS</u>

then slice off sections

Prepare the feathers so they can be installed with light pressure.

in place. Next, hold the second part of the trough in place and set the two braces (E) so you can locate their positions. Apply glue to all mating surfaces; install no. 8 × 1½″ flathead screws through the trough-part into the brace and two no. 6 × 1″ flathead screws through the bottom of the guide. Before finalizing the assembly, use a square or triangle to be sure the angle between the trough-parts is 90°.

USING THE JIG

Mating parts, already miter cut, are held in the jig by hand or with clamps as the jig is moved past the saw blade. Use a stop block, clamped to the jig, to gauge the location of the cuts. Make the same cut on all parts before changing the position of the stop block to gauge other cuts. Adjust the projection of the saw blade so it cuts about three-quarters of the way into the miter joint.

Most saw blades will produce a ⅛″-wide kerf so materials like ply-

wood or hardboard can be used for feathers. Make the cuts with a dadoing tool if the project calls for thicker feathers.

CUSTOM-MADE FEATHERS

A good way to make feathers is to cut off a corner of a piece of stock and then slice it into individual pieces. Be sure the parent stock is long enough for safe handling.

In all cases, prepare the feathers so they are a bit wider and longer than needed so they can be trimmed and sanded flush after assembly.

Table Saw Master Jig

When the blade's projection is enough for ¾″ stock, the master jig has more than enough capacity to crosscut 12″-wide material.

Paint the inserts a bright yellow to point up the "danger zone." Always use the guard even though it isn't shown in all the photos.

The master jig is one of the most popular shop-made accessories for the table saw. This is a do-anything jig that incorporates a cluster of modules, each of which you are likely to need at some time for convenience, accuracy, production output, and increased safety on routine, and some not so routine

applications. *Popular Woodworking* magazine presented the original concept in the January 1994 issue. Since that time, the jig, which is on my machine more than it is off, has been modified to the point where it seemed wise to rebuild it from scratch.

The "new" jig retains the practical aspects of the original project but

with additions and improvements, including:

- easier-to-produce table inserts for use with a saw blade or dado tool,
- a more professional fence with a built-in adjustable stop,
- a redesigned, more flexible tenoning attachment that includes a

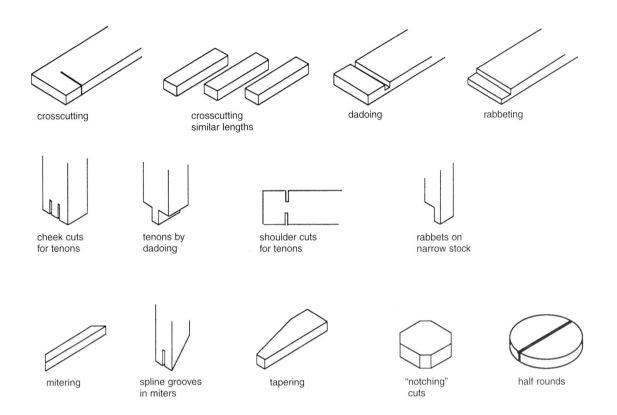

crosscutting

crosscutting
similar lengths

dadoing

rabbeting

cheek cuts
for tenons

tenons by
dadoing

shoulder cuts
for tenons

rabbets on
narrow stock

mitering

spline grooves
in miters

tapering

"notching"
cuts

half rounds

Use the adjustable stop to cut parts of similar length. Capacity to the left of the blade is about 22″. Don't over-tighten the locking thumb screw; slight pressure will secure the stop-slide. Avoid sawing into the stop-slide by limiting blade projection to just enough to saw through 1½″ material.

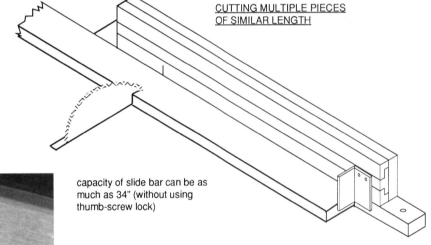

CUTTING MULTIPLE PIECES
OF SIMILAR LENGTH

capacity of slide bar can be as much as 34″ (without using thumb-screw lock)

Form dadoes and rabbets with the jig in crosscut mode. Use the adjustable stop when the same cut is required in several pieces. *Do not* have the regular dado insert installed in the saw table when using the master jig for dado work.

Use the V-shaped guide when miter-sawing frame parts that have been precut to length. Check the position of the guide in relation to the saw blade with a square or draftsman's template before tightening the lock bolts.

swiveling guide so, for example, forming spline grooves in miter cuts is not limited to those of 45°,

- a tapering jig,
- and thoughts on how to add "notching jigs" for producing odd-shaped components or making cuts that might not be safe to do by conventional means.

The principle advantage of the project is that it is essentially a sliding table. All the components are secured to the main table so that regardless of the operation—crosscutting, mitering, dadoing, tapering, forming tenons or grooves in miter cuts for splines or feathers—the work and the jig move together. This eliminates the

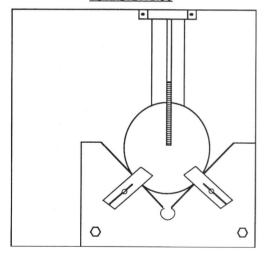

A unique application—use the V-shaped miter guide to halve or quarter discs. Secure the work with the hold-downs.

Use the triangular miter guide when making consecutive cuts with a single length of stock. Both mitering guides allow left- and right-hand cuts, so working with molding is no problem.

friction normally present when work contacts the saw's table directly, and it minimizes the amount of hand pressure that must be applied to the work to secure it while making cuts.

When making miter cuts, special guides on the master jig eliminate "creep," the accuracy-spoiling bugaboo that is always present when doing such work with just the miter gauge. When doing tenoning operations with either a saw blade or dadoing tool, the work is held securely in the jig's tenoning accessory. This improves accuracy and is much safer than hand-holding narrow stock on edge while moving it along the rip fence. Even simple crosscutting is easier and more accurate because the jig's fence gives more sup-

Have the blade at its highest projection when you install the tenoning jig and bring the face of the jig flush against the blade. Do this before tightening the guide-bar bolts to be sure the jig's face and the saw blade are parallel.

The swivel guide is used as a vertical guide when making cheek cuts for a tenon. Use a square to be sure the angle between the bearing edge of the guide and the table is 90°. Use a 5/16″ carriage bolt through the guide's pivot hole, and a 1/4″ carriage bolt through the groove.

Make cheek cuts for tenons with the work positioned so the waste falls away from the saw blade. Note the use of the hold-down. Use a piece of scrap between the hold-down and the face of the jig. Alternately, use a clamp to secure the work.

A dadoing tool speeds up the chore of forming tenons, since it eliminates having to make shoulder cuts. When a second cut is made after flipping the stock, the tenon will be centered.

Use one of the tenoning jig's miter guides when forming spline grooves in miter cuts. Mark one surface of all parts involved and place that surface against the face of the jig for all cuts. Thus, the grooves will match even if the groove isn't exactly centered.

Use both of the miter guides when forming grooves for feathers. Again, mark the same surface of all parts and have that surface against the face of the jig when sawing.

The swivel guide can be set to accommodate angles other than 45°. The guide can be positioned using any of the top holes in the jig, and it can also be inverted.

port than the face of a miter gauge.

Overall, the master jig hosts a collection of essential, but usually separate, jigs and provides the advantages of a sliding table for each of them. Typical chores that can be accomplished with the master jig are shown on page 25.

CONSTRUCTION

The master jig in my shop is sized for a 10″ Delta Unisaw which has a 27″ × 28¼″ table. Many 9″ and 10″ machines—the most popular sizes—are similar, so the dimensions in the drawings and the materials list may be applicable without drastic changes. Anyway, check for necessary conversions before cutting material.

The thickness of the jig's table reduces the maximum projection of the saw blade, but since a 10″ blade will project 3″ or more above the table, the reduction is not critical. An 8″ or 9″ can be used with the jig for many woodworking jobs. But for dadoing, it's necessary to use an 8″ unit to allow the blades to extend a practical amount above the slot.

Accurate construction is important, although some tolerances are built in. For example, the fastening holes in the attachments are ⅜″ in diameter even though they are secured with 5⁄16″ bolts that thread into the threaded inserts that are installed in the table. This allows for minor alignment adjustments when putting the attachments in place. Because of possible human error, the ⅜″ holes can be enlarged an additional 1⁄16″.

IN GENERAL

Careful attention to all details of construction is essential for the master jig to perform efficiently. The project is a lifetime shop accessory and will be on your table saw, as mine is, more often than it is stored. So taking adequate time and previewing each construction step before performing it makes sense.

Sand all components before and after assembly. Apply two (or more) coats of sanding sealer to all surfaces and edges, sanding between coats and after the final one. An occasional application of paste wax, rubbed to a polish, to the saw's table and the underside of the sliding table is a good idea.

This is a typical notching jig in use. In this case, the part being removed is waste. The hold-down is one that is used with the table's miter guides. Secure the hold-down with a round head screw.

Using the taper jig. Use a hold-down so hands can be free of the cut area. A special jig can be made for a job that can't be handled by the example taper jig.

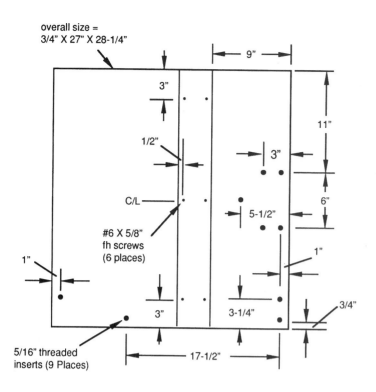

overall size =
3/4" X 27" X 28-1/4"

9"

3"

11"

1/2"

3"

6"

C/L

5-1/2"

#6 X 5/8"
fh screws
(6 places)

1"

1"

1"

3"

3-1/4"

3/4"

5/16" threaded
inserts (9 Places)

17-1/2"

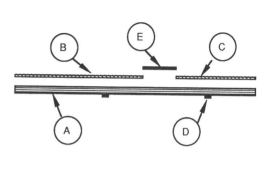

MATERIALS LIST				
TABLE SAW MASTER JIG				
Table				
QTY.	KEY	NAME	SIZE (IN INCHES)	MATERIAL
1	A	Base	$\frac{1}{2} \times 27 \times 28\frac{1}{4}$	Plywood
1	B	Top Left	$\frac{1}{4} \times 15\frac{1}{2} \times 27$	Plywood
1	C	Top Right	$\frac{1}{4} \times 9 \times 27$	Plywood
2	D	Guide Bar	$\frac{3}{8} \times \frac{3}{4} \times 27$	Hardwood
2	E	Insert	$\frac{1}{4} \times 3\frac{3}{4} \times 27$	Plywood
No. 6 × ⅝″ Flathead Screw (6)			$\frac{5}{16}$″ Threaded Insert (9)	

MAKING THE JIG

STEP 1 : THE MAIN TABLE

Cut the base and the top left and right parts to size and join them with contact cement. To prevent the cement from messing the space between the top parts, outline the open area with strips of masking tape. I decided on this assembly because it makes it easy to provide for the removable inserts. The original one-piece table required

some precise router work to form a recess for the inserts.

STEP 2: INSTALL THE THREADED INSERTS

Carefully lay out the location of all the inserts that must be installed in the table. Spot their locations with a center punch and drill $\frac{1}{16}$″ pilot holes. Enlarge the holes to $\frac{1}{2}$″ diameter, drilling from the top surface and using a backup block on the underside.

The holes are close enough to the edges of the table so the drilling can be done on a drill press to ensure squareness. Install the threaded inserts through the bottom of the table until they are almost flush with the table's surface.

STEP 3: ADD THE GUIDE BARS

Shape the hardwood guide bars so they will ride smoothly and without wobble in the miter gauge slots of your machine. Set the bars in position on the saw and then place the jig's table so its left side and front edge are aligned with the same edges on the saw's table.

Use slim brads at each end and at a center point to tack-nail through the jig's table to keep the bars in correct position. Attach both bars permanently with three no. 6 × ⅞″ flathead screws through the underside of the bars. Drill shank and pilot holes and countersink for the screws. If you don't do this, the screws might spread the bars too tightly in the table slots.

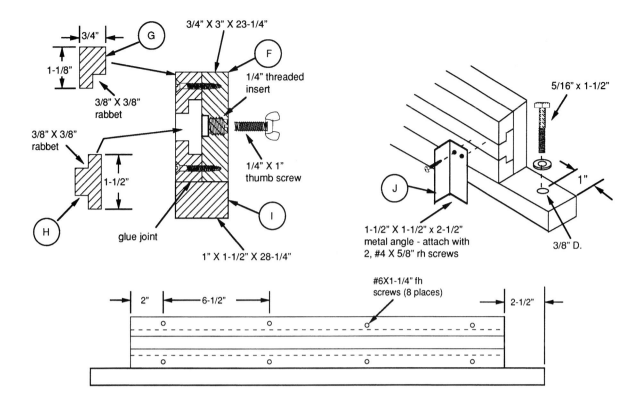

STEP 4: MAKE THE INSERTS

Cut several inserts to the size called for in the materials list and mark the location of the attachment screws on one of them. Clamp the pieces together as a pad, and, with the marked one serving as a template, drill through them for the six no. $6 \times \frac{5}{8}''$ flathead screws. Install one insert,

countersinking carefully, so the screws will be flush with the table's surface.

STEP 5: FORM THE INITIAL SAW KERF

Use a good saw blade, preferably a high-quality carbide-tipped combination blade that will always be used with the jig. With the machine shut

down, lower the blade so it is below the table, and then use a clamp or two to secure the sliding table in correct position. Turn on the machine and slowly raise the blade until it cuts through the insert. Remove the clamps and advance the table to lengthen the kerf to about 12″. An exact kerf-length is not critical at this point.

Repeat the procedure with a second insert to form a dado slot through both the sliding table and the insert. Actually, you can do this later, at some time when you need to work with a dadoing tool. A point to make—when you use the jig for dadoing work, *do not* have the regular dado insert in place in the machine.

MAKING THE FENCE

STEP 1: PREPARE THE BACK

Cut the back (F) to exact size and then install the ¼″ threaded insert for

MATERIALS LIST				
TABLE SAW MASTER JIG **Fence**				
QTY.	KEY	NAME	SIZE (IN INCHES)	MATERIAL
1	F	Back	¾ × 3 × 23¼	Hardwood
2	G	Retainer	¾ × 1⅛ × 23¼	Hardwood
1	H	Slide Bar	¾ × 1½ × 23¼	Hardwood
1	I	Base	1 × 1½ × 28¼	Hardwood
1	J	Stop	1½ × 1½ × 2½	Metal Angle

No. 6 × 1¼″ Flathead Screw (8)

¼″ Threaded Insert (1)

¼″ × 1″ Thumb Screw (1)

No. 4 × ⅝″ Round Head Screw (2)

5⁄16″ × 1½″ Bolt with Washer (2)

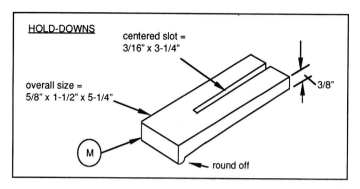

HOLD-DOWNS

overall size = 5/8" x 1-1/2" x 5-1/4"

centered slot = 3/16" x 3-1/4"

3/8"

round off

M

NOTE -- install 3/16" threaded inserts, two places in each guide. Use 3/16" X 1" rh screws to secure hold-downs

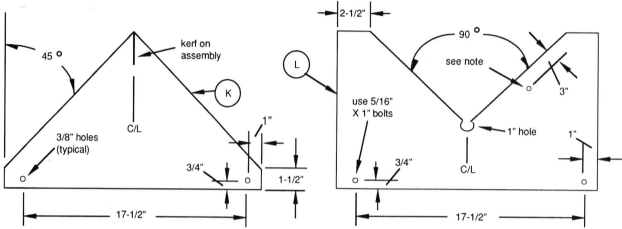

45°

kerf on assembly

K

C/L

3/8" holes (typical)

1"

3/4"

1-1/2"

17-1/2"

2-1/2"

90°

see note

L

use 5/16" X 1" bolts

3"

1" hole

3/4"

C/L

1"

17-1/2"

---

the thumb screw that locks the slide bar (H). Locate the insert about 3″ to the left of the kerf in the table.

STEP 2: MAKE THE RETAINERS AND SLIDE BAR

For the retainers (G), start with a piece that is twice as long as the materials list calls for. After forming the ⅜″ × ⅜″ rabbet, halve the piece to get the two parts that are needed.

Prepare the slide bar (H) to exact size and then make the rabbet cut along both edges. The rabbet cuts in the retainers and the slide bar can be formed with a dadoing tool or by making two passes with a saw blade. These are slim pieces, so use a push stick to get them past the cutter.

STEP 3: ASSEMBLE RETAINERS AND BACK

Attach the bottom retainer to the back with four no. 6 × 1¼″ flathead screws. Then, using the slide bar for positioning, add the top retainer in the same way. If necessary, do some judicious sanding on the slide bar so it will move easily.

STEP 4: ADD THE BASE AND STOP

Cut the base (I) to size, and after drilling the ⅜″ holes at each end, add it to the fence by gluing and clamping. The final chore is to attach the stop (J), which is a piece of steel or aluminum angle, to the end of the slide bar. Use small thin washers between the angle and the bar so the stop won't rub against the retainers.

QTY.	KEY	NAME	SIZE (IN INCHES)	MATERIAL
MATERIALS LIST				
TABLE SAW MASTER JIG				
Miter Guides				
1	K	Tri-Guide	½ × 11½ × 20	Plywood
1	L	V-Guide	½ × 11½ × 20	Plywood
2	M	Hold-Down	⅝ × 1½ × 5¼	Hardwood
³⁄₁₆″ Threaded Insert (4)			⁵⁄₁₆″ × 1″ Bolt (2)	
³⁄₁₆″ × 1″ Round Head Screw (2)				

tenoning jig
face layout

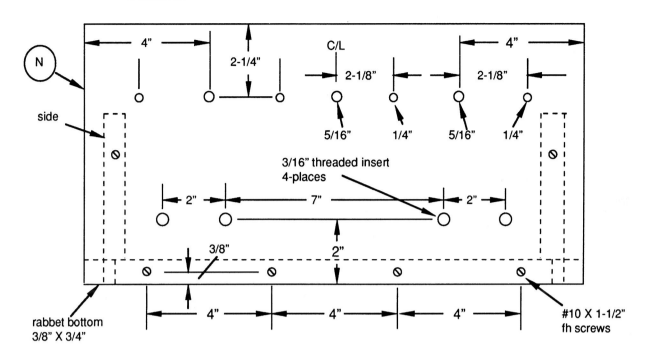

MAKING THE MITER GUIDES

STEP 1: PREPARE THE GUIDES

The triangular guide (K) is used when making miter cuts consecutively on a piece of stock that is long enough to supply all or some of the parts that are required. Use the V-shaped guide

(L) when the frame components have been precut to length.

Prepare the stock for both guides to overall size and then, in turn, bolt them in place on the sliding table. Place a straightedge flush against the left side of the saw blade and mark along the straightedge to establish a line on the guide. Assuming the blade

cuts a ⅛" kerf, the true centerline on the guide will be 1/16" to the right of the marked line.

Work from the centerline with a combination square or a draftsman's template to establish the 45° angles on each of the guides. It's a good idea to saw close to the lines and then finish by sanding.

MATERIALS LIST				
TABLE SAW MASTER JIG				
Tenoning Jig				
QTY.	KEY	NAME	SIZE (IN INCHES)	MATERIAL
1	N	Face	¾ × 8 × 16½	Hardwood
1	O	Base	¾ × 7¾ × 14	Hardwood
2	P	Side	¾ × 5¼ × 7″	Hardwood
2	Q	Guide	¾ × 1 × 5	Hardwood
³⁄₁₆″ Threaded Insert (4)			⁵⁄₁₆″ × 1¼″ Bolt (2)	
No. 10 × 1½″ Flathead Screw (8)				

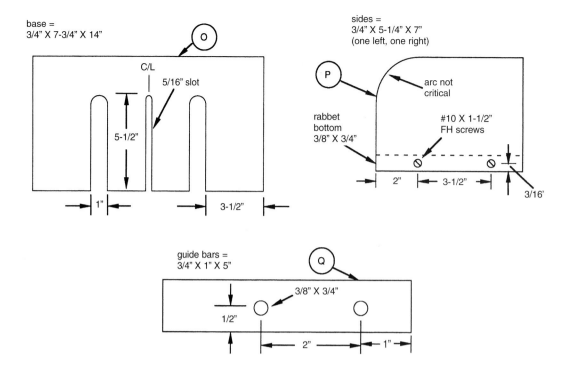

base =
3/4" X 7-3/4" X 14"

O

C/L

5/16" slot

5-1/2"

1"

3-1/2"

sides =
3/4" X 5-1/4" X 7"
(one left, one right)

P

arc not
critical

rabbet
bottom
3/8" X 3/4"

#10 X 1-1/2"
FH screws

2"

3-1/2"

3/16'

guide bars =
3/4" X 1" X 5"

Q

3/8" X 3/4"

1/2"

2"

1"

STEP 2: INSTALL THE INSERTS

The location of the inserts is at a mid-point along the 45° sides, and 3" from the cut edge. Drill for the inserts from the bottom of the guides and then install them so they are almost flush with the top surface.

STEP 3: MAKE THE HOLD-DOWNS

The hold-downs (M) that are secured with ³⁄₁₆″ × 1″ round head screws are simple, but they work. Form the slot by first drilling a ³⁄₁₆″ hole where the slot ends, and then remove the waste with a scroll saw or band saw or even a hand saw.

MAKING THE TENONING JIG

STEP 1: MAKE THE FACE

Cut the part (N) to size and carefully lay out the locations of all the holes. The top line of holes (either ¼″ or

⁵⁄₁₆″) are through-holes that are needed for the swivel guide. The remaining four holes are bored for the ³⁄₁₆″ threaded inserts that are used when working with the tenoning jig's miter guides.

After all the holes are drilled and the threaded inserts are installed, rabbet the bottom edge of the face ³⁄₈″-deep × ¾″-wide to accept the ¾″ base.

STEP 2: BASE, SIDES AND GUIDE BARS

Cut the base (O) to size and lay out the centerlines for the three slots. Bore end-holes and then clean away the waste by making saw cuts. The center ⁵⁄₁₆″ slot allows the jig to be moved in relation to the saw blade. A ⁵⁄₁₆″ × 1¼″ bolt that threads into the threaded insert that is in the sliding table secures adjustments.

To produce the sides (P), start with a piece that is more than 14″ long. Then, after forming the ³⁄₈″-deep × ¾″-wide rabbet along one edge, saw

the part to get two pieces. Remember, when you round off one of the top corners, that these are left- and right-hand parts.

Next, do a dry assembly of the three components (face, base and sides) to be sure the angle between the face and base is 90°. When you're certain of the alignment, assemble the parts with glue and no. 10 × 1½″ flathead screws.

The guide bars (Q), which are secured with ⁵⁄₁₆″ bolts that thread into the inserts in the sliding table, are straightforward pieces, but be sure their width is exactly 1″.

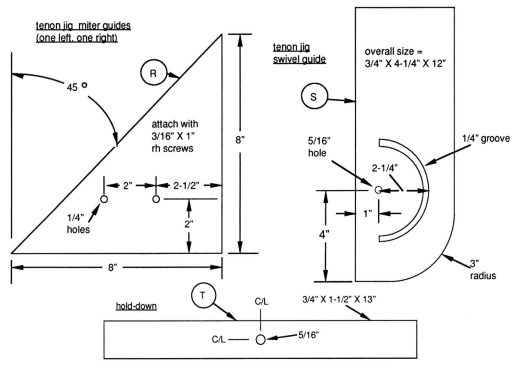

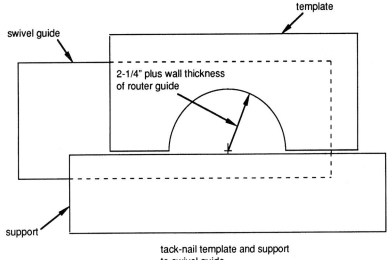

tack-nail template and support
to swivel guide

TENONING JIG ATTACHMENTS

STEP 1: MITER GUIDES

The miter guides (R) that are used with the tenoning jig are triangular pieces with 8″ sides. Although they are secured to the jig's face with ³⁄₁₆″ screws, the attachment holes are ¼″. This allows for adjustment when the guides are secured to the jig's face.

STEP 2: MAKE THE SWIVEL GUIDE

Prepare the part for the guide (S) and then form the ¼″-wide, semicircular groove. This can be done by drilling end-holes and removing the waste with a scroll saw or with a coping saw, but results will be better if you form the groove by working with a portable router that is equipped with a pivot guide. Another solution is to establish the setup that is detailed in the drawing at mid page. This calls for a router equipped with a template guide that will follow the semicircular cutout

MATERIALS LIST				
TABLE SAW MASTER JIG **Tenoning Jig Attachments**				
QTY.	KEY	NAME	SIZE (IN INCHES)	MATERIAL
2	R	Guide	¼×8×8	Plywood
1	S	Swivel Guide	¾×4¼×12	Hardwood
1	T	Hold-Down	¾×1½×13	Hardwood

³⁄₁₆″ × 1″ Round Head Screw (4)

⁵⁄₁₆″ × 2″ Carriage Bolt with Washer and Wing Nut (1)

¼″ × 2″ Carriage Bolt with Washer and Wing Nut (1)

¼″ × 2½″ Carriage Bolt with Washer and Wing Nut (1)

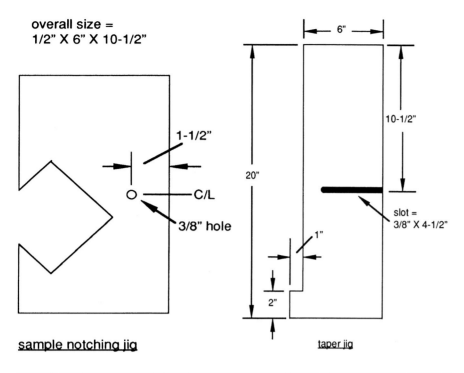

overall size =
1/2" X 6" X 10-1/2"

1-1/2"

C/L

3/8" hole

sample notching jig

6"

10-1/2"

20"

1"

2"

slot =
3/8" X 4-1/2"

taper jig

MATERIALS LIST				
TABLE SAW MASTER JIG				
Guard And Support				
QTY.	KEY	NAME	SIZE (IN INCHES)	MATERIAL
1	U	Support	$1\frac{1}{2} \times 4 \times 8$	Hardwood
1	V	Guard	$\frac{1}{4} \times 5 \times 28$	Acrylic
No. $8 \times 1\frac{1}{2}''$ Round Head Screw (2)			No. $8 \times 1''$ Round Head Screw (2)	

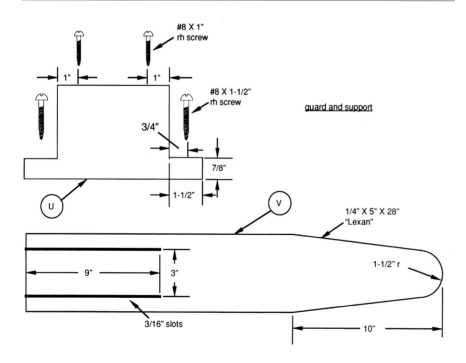

#8 X 1"
rh screw

1"   1"

#8 X 1-1/2"
rh screw

3/4"

7/8"

1-1/2"

guard and support

U

V

1/4" X 5" X 28"
"Lexan"

1-1/2" r

9"

3"

3/16" slots

10"

that is in the template. In either case, make repeat passes, projecting the bit an extra ⅛" or so for each one.

NOTCHING AND TAPER JIGS

Notching jigs must be custom-designed for particular applications. The cutout in the jig can fit the part that is needed or the section that must be removed from the component.

The taper jig, as designed, is pretty flexible and is useful for many taper-cutting chores. Actually, it's feasible to make special ones when it's necessary to produce many duplicate parts.

Notching jigs and the taper jig are locked in place by using the same threaded insert that's installed in the sliding table to secure the tenoning jig.

DON'T FORGET THE GUARD

STEP 1: MAKE THE SUPPORT

Cut the part (U) to overall size, and then work on a band saw or scroll saw to form the L-shaped notch at each end. Install the support so it and the kerf in the sliding table will have a common centerline.

STEP 2: MAKE THE GUARD

I used Lexan but any clear, rigid plastic will do. The guard (V) spans across the table when doing crosscutting and dado work, but the slots allow other positions that might be more suitable when using the table's miter guides, for example. Form the slots (as I suggested for other parts) by drilling end-holes and then sawing away the waste.

The Column Jig

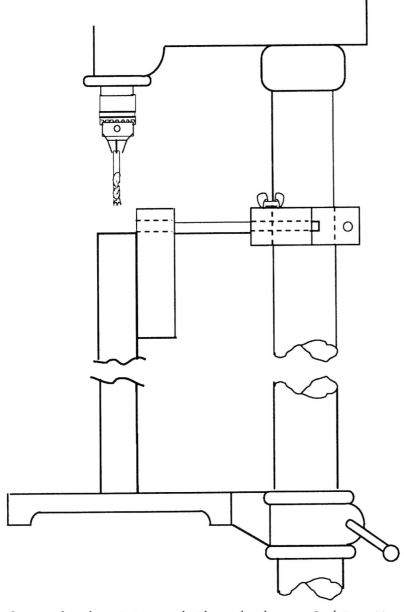

Drilling accurate end-holes in long stock is chancy without a setup that guarantees the bit will enter the wood at right angles to the surface. The column jig, consisting of a bracket that locks to the drill press column and an adjustable fence against which the work is hand-held or clamped, solves the problem. The bottom edge of the work rests on the tool's table.

The jig is ideal for a floor-model machine because of the capacity between chuck and table, but it can also serve many purposes on a bench-top model, and capacity can be increased somewhat by using the base of the tool as a proxy table. There is also the traditional method of getting more from a "small" tool. Swing the head of the drill press so it projects beyond the bench. Thus, capacity is from the chuck to the floor.

The fence on the column jig is secured with two thumb screws. Lock its position so holes in the work will have the edge-distance that is needed. The jig is vertically adjustable so it can be positioned to provide the most suitable support for the work.

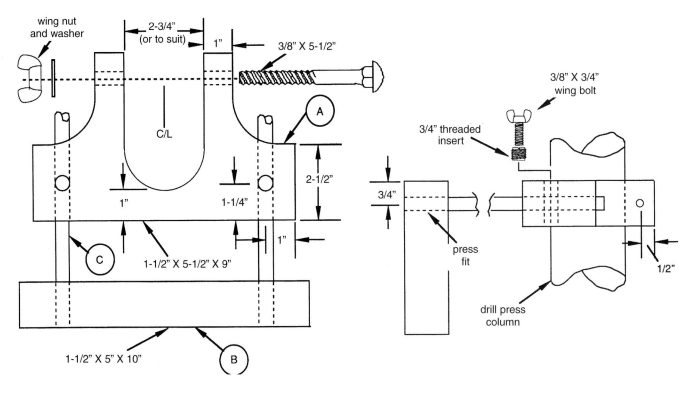

Construction details for the column jig. The round-end slot is sized to suit the diameter of the tool's column.

MATERIALS LIST				
DRILL PRESS COLUMN JIG				
QTY.	KEY	NAME	SIZE (IN INCHES)	MATERIAL
1	A	Bracket	1½×5½×9	Hardwood
1	B	Fence	1½×5×10	Hardwood
2	C	Guide	½×9	Steel Rod
⅜″×5½″ Carriage Bolt with Wing Nut and Washer (1)			⅜″ Threaded Insert (2)	
			⅜″×¾″ Wing Bolt (2)	

MAKING THE JIG

STEP 1: START WITH THE BRACKET

Cut the bracket (A) to size and mark a centerline across its width and down the adjacent edge. Mark the locations of the holes for the two threaded inserts and, in the edge of the part, the locations for the two guides (C). The holes for the inserts can be through, or you can limit depth to about ¾″. Those for the guides must be at least 2½″ deep. It's best to drill these holes before shaping the bracket to final form.

Shape the outside edges of the bracket on a band saw or scroll saw and smooth the sawed edges with a drum sander. Next, drill the hole for the carriage bolt. Do this on the drill press by resting the part on a block of wood. You may have to drill from both sides unless you have a bit that's long enough to pass through the

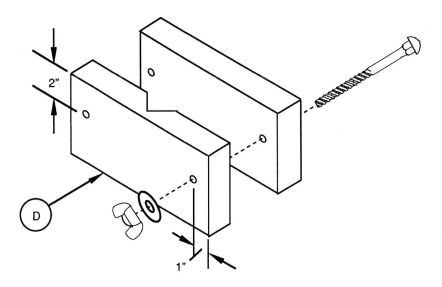

The V-block is a handy attachment. Locate the holes through block and fence to avoid interference from the jig's guide bars.

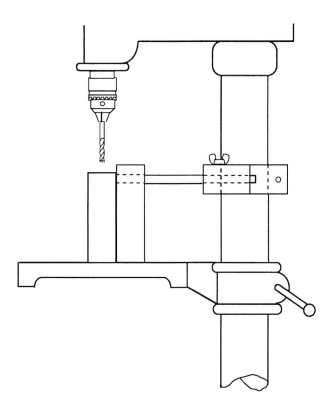

Drilling holes on a common centerline into the edge of narrow stock is another chore for which the jig provides accuracy. Work and fence can rest on the tool's table when the width of the work is not greater than that of the fence.

stock. If so, the holes don't have to be more than about 1"-deep.

Start the slot in the bracket by using a fly cutter or a hole saw to form a hole that suits the diameter of the drill press column, then saw out the waste. Alternately, form the slot on a band saw or scroll saw and smooth the cut edges with a drum sander. However you work, size the width of the slot for a snug fit with the tool's column.

Install the two ⅜" threaded inserts.

STEP 2: MAKE THE FENCE

Cut the part (B) to size and drill the holes for the guides. Be sure the holes mate directly with the holes that are already in the bracket. Holes that are slightly undersize will provide a tight fit for the guides, but for extra security, coat the ends of the guides with epoxy before tapping them into place.

STEP 3: MAKE A V-BLOCK

The size of the block (D) equals that of the fence. Form the V down the center of the block and about 1⅛"-deep. Drill the holes for the carriage bolts while the fence and V-block are held together. Actually, it's better to do this before installing the guide bars in the fence.

USING THE JIG

The fence is adjusted for whatever hole edge-distance is needed. Clamp a strip of wood to the fence as a stop when the same hole is required on multiple components. The drill press stop rod is used in normal fashion to control the depth of the holes.

The jig is also available for controlling edge-distance when drilling a series of holes into the edge of narrow stock. In this case, both the fence and the work will rest on the table.

Use the V-block setup when drilling concentric holes in round stock, as shown in the drawing.

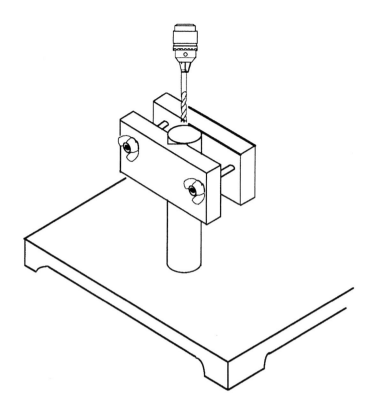

The V-block positions round stock so concentric holes can be drilled accurately.

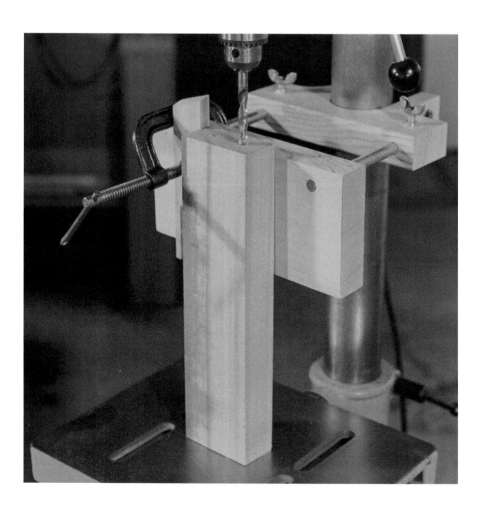

Adjustable V-Block

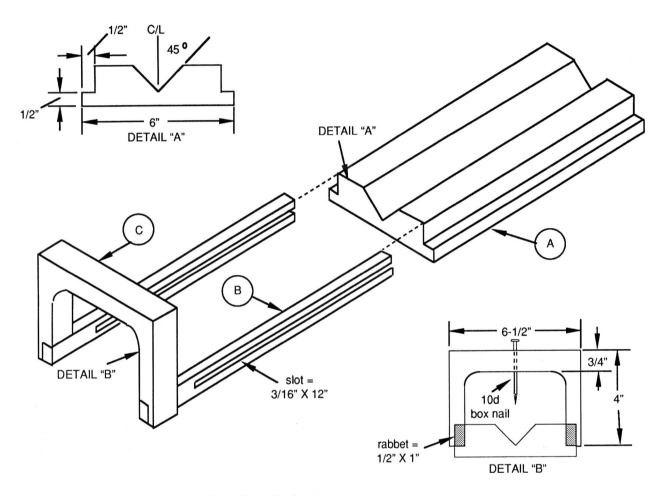

DETAIL "A"

1/2"   C/L
45°
1/2"
6"

DETAIL "B"

slot =
3/16" X 12"

6-1/2"
3/4"
4"
10d
box nail
rabbet =
1/2" X 1"

Construction details for the drill press adjustable V-block.

Drilling holes accurately on the diameter of round components or materials like tubing can be challenging without a setup that will position and hold the work correctly. A simple V-block is a common solution, but the more ad-vanced version that is detailed in the drawing below is more functional. The nail-guide keeps the work from rotating so a series of holes will be on the same centerline, and it can serve as a gauge when the holes must be equally spaced.

MAKING THE JIG

STEP 1 : MAKE THE BODY

The edge-rabbets can be formed by using the two-pass method—the first cut with the stock flat on the table, the second one with the stock on edge. Place the stock for the second pass so the waste falls away from the saw blade.

Alternately, make the cuts in a single pass by using a dado that is set to cut a bit more than ½"-wide.

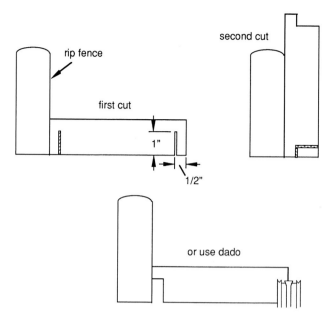

Make the rabbet cuts in the body by using the two-pass method or by making a single pass with a dadoing tool.

MATERIALS LIST				
SELF-CENTERING V-BLOCK				
QTY.	KEY	NAME	SIZE (IN INCHES)	MATERIAL
1	D	Block	1½ × 5 × 10	Hardwood
⅜" × 6" Carriage Bolt with Wing Nut and Washer (2)				
V-BLOCK JIG				
QTY.	KEY	NAME	SIZE (IN INCHES)	MATERIAL
1	A	Body	1½ × 6 × 12	Hardwood
2	B	Slide	½ × 1 × 14	Hardwood
1	C	Guide	1½ × 4 × 6½	Hardwood
No. 9 × 1¼" Round Head Screw with Washer (2)		10d Box Nail (1)		

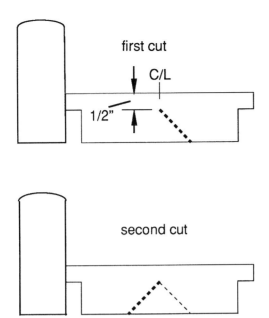

first cut

C/L

1/2"

second cut

Be sure the bottom of the V is on the centerline of the body.

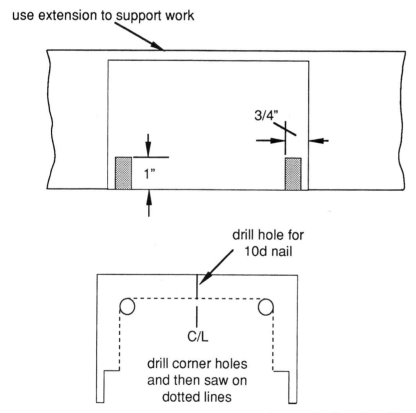

use extension to support work

3/4"

1"

drill hole for
10d nail

C/L

drill corner holes
and then saw on
dotted lines

Be sure to use a miter gauge extension when making the cuts that form the rabbets in the guide.

STEP 2: FORM THE V-GROOVE

Make the first pass by tilting the saw blade to 45° and setting the rip fence so the kerf will be on the centerline of the work. Then, turn the work end-for-end and make a second pass. For this step, use a pusher to move the work, and do not stand in line with the blade; the waste piece may be captured by the blade and thrown back toward the operator.

STEP 3: MAKE THE GUIDE

Prepare the part (C) to overall size and make a layout that will show the position of the rabbet cuts and the internal shape. Set a dado so it will cut ½"-wide and 1"-deep and make the two cuts. For accuracy and safety, make the cuts with the work clamped to a miter gauge extension.

Drill two ½" corner holes and then saw out the waste by working on a band saw or scroll saw.

STEP 4: PREPARE THE SLIDES

Cut the slides (B) to size and drill a ³⁄₁₆" hole to mark the end of the slot. These are slim pieces, so don't try to remove the waste on a table saw. Instead, do the chore on a scroll saw or band saw.

Attach the slides to the guide with glue and a couple of ⅝" brads.

USING THE JIG

Clamp the jig on the drill press table so the drill bit is on the center of the V. For a series of equally spaced holes, drill the first one, and then position the guide so the nail engages the first hole to establish the spacing.

The jig is usually used to drill pilot holes that can then be enlarged. Use the jig for enlarging the holes to be sure the "new" hole follows the path of the first one.

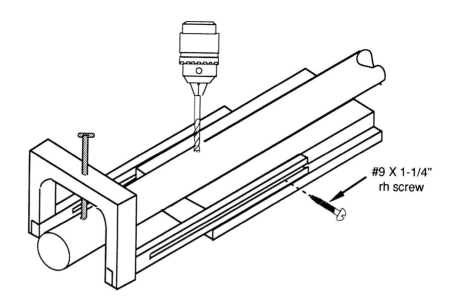

#9 X 1-1/4" rh screw

To drill a series of equally spaced holes, position the guide so the pin will engage the last hole that was drilled. Secure the position of the guide/slide assembly with round head screws.

An Auxiliary Tilting Table

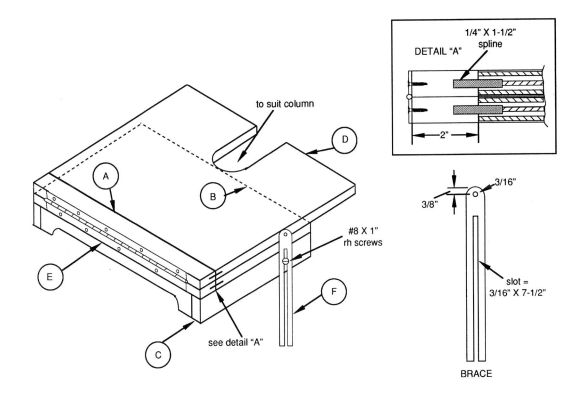

DETAIL "A"

1/4" X 1-1/2" spline

2"

to suit column

D

A

B

#8 X 1"
rh screws

E

C

see detail "A"

F

3/16"

3/8"

slot =
3/16" X 7-1/2"

BRACE

Construction details for the drill press tilt jig. Check the materials list for the size of components.

Drill press tables tilt left or right (if at all) on a plane that is perpendicular to the quill—a design that doesn't contribute to accuracy or convenience—especially on long stock, when drilling holes at an angle to the work's surface. So, my answer is a jig with an adjustable table that tilts forward. It's also possible to combine the tilt feature of the jig with that of the machine's table to drill compound angle holes. My project suits a Delta 7½" drill press with an 11" × 14" table, but the concept is easily adaptable for any machine.

MAKING THE JIG

STEP 1 : MAKE THE TABLES

Screws don't hold very well in edges of plywood, so I use wood strips on the front edge of the tables so the screws for the piano hinge will have something to bite into.

Start by preparing the base (B), the tilt unit (D) and the edge-pieces (A). Mark a centerline on the tilt unit and lay out the shape of the round-end slot so it suits the diameter of the tool's column. Make the slot long enough so the tilt unit can lay flat without interference from the col-

umn. Use a fly cutter or hole saw to form an end-hole and then saw out the waste on a band saw or scroll saw.

STEP 2: JOIN THE PARTS (DETAIL "A")

Set up a dado so it will form a groove ¼"-wide by ¾"-deep and cut grooves in the mating edges of the four parts. If you mark the same surface on each of the pieces and have that surface against the rip fence when cutting, it won't matter if the grooves are not exactly centered. But those same surfaces must face up or down when assembling.

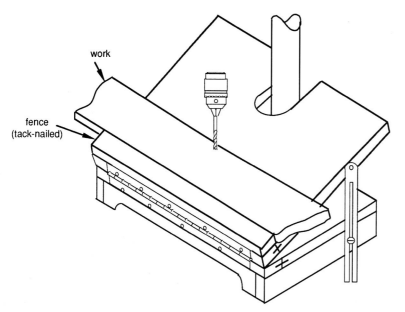

work

fence
(tack-nailed)

A strip of wood will serve as a fence to hold the position of the work when drilling a series of holes that must have the same edge-distance.

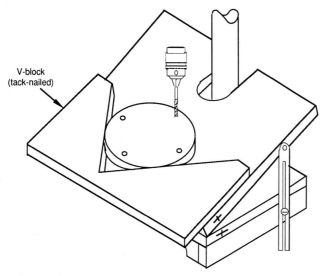

V-block
(tack-nailed)

Using a V-block to position work when drilling holes on a circular path.

MATERIALS LIST				
DRILL PRESS TILT JIG				
QTY.	KEY	NAME	SIZE (IN INCHES)	MATERIAL
2	A	End Piece	¾ × 2 × 15½	Optional
1	B	Base	¾ × 9 × 15½	Plywood
2	C	Clamp Ledge	¾ × 1½ × 11	Optional
1	D	Tilt Unit	¾ × 13½ × 15½	Plywood
1	E	Hinge	¾ × ¾ × 14	Piano Hinge
2	F	Brace	¼ × 1 × 8	Hardboard
2		Spline	¼ × 1½ × 15½	Optional
No. 8 × 1″ Round Head Screw (4)			Flathead Screws For Hinge	

Prepare the splines, using wood, plywood or hardboard, and after coating contact areas with glue, hold the parts together with clamps until the glue sets.

STEP 3: ADD THE CLAMP LEDGES AND THE HINGE

Cut the ledges (C) to size and attach them to the base with glue and 6d finishing nails. Hold the parts together with clamps before driving the nails and check to be sure the assembly fits nicely on the drill press table.

Place the base-assembly and the tilt unit on the table and secure them with clamps while you attach the piano hinge.

STEP 4: MAKE THE BRACE

Cut the parts to size, and form the slot by first drilling a ³⁄₁₆″ end-hole and then sawing out the waste on a scroll saw or band saw. Round off the top end of the brace and attach it so it doesn't project above the surface of the tilt unit.

USING THE JIG

Tack-nail a strip of wood at the front edge of the table to serve as a fence when drilling a series of holes on a common centerline (see top drawing at left). The width of the work may require placing the fence at the back end of the tilt unit. If so, hand-hold or use a spring clamp to prevent the work from sliding out of position. Establish the angle between the table and the drill bit with a T-bevel.

Special setups can be used for particular drilling chores. For example, use a V-block to position work when drilling angular holes in a circular component (see bottom drawing at left). Place the V-block so its center and the drill bit are on a common centerline.

The Master Jig for the Drill Press

The drill press master jig with some of its accessories. The drawers provide storage space for items like sanding drums, bits, rotary cutters, and so on. It isn't necessary to make all the "add-ons" immediately. Start with the table and add other units at your own pace.

The drill press is one of the most versatile tools in a woodworking shop. I feel, as many others do, that it's the second machine to acquire after a sawing tool. Nothing proves the thought more than the master jig. The project outfits the drill press for many routine and some not-so-routine operations: drilling, drum sanding, routing, shaping, drilling and sanding pivot-guided circular components, pin routing and

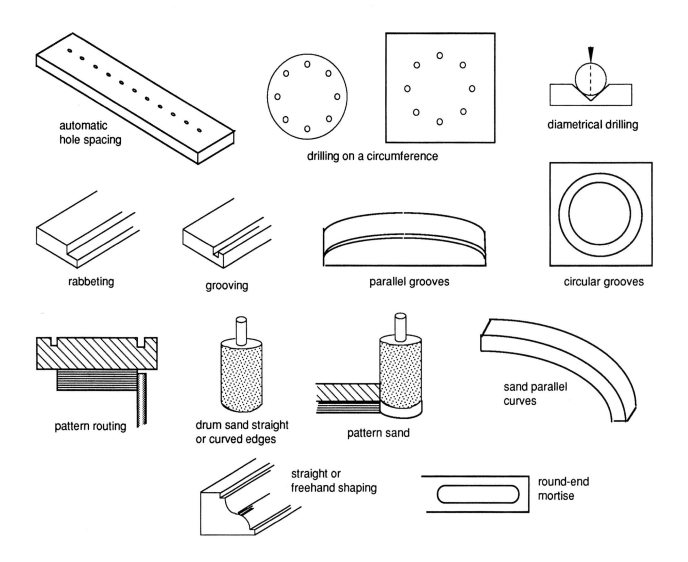

automatic hole spacing

drilling on a circumference

diametrical drilling

rabbeting

grooving

parallel grooves

circular grooves

pattern routing

drum sand straight or curved edges

pattern sand

sand parallel curves

straight or freehand shaping

round-end mortise

more (see examples above). Some of the chores can't be done conveniently any other way.

The truth is, the design of the master jig evolved from previous ideas and from a simpler version that I put together for efficient drum sanding and drum sander storage. The drill press is great for such work, but the regular table won't do. For drum sanding only, you don't need more than an inverted U-shaped structure with a hole at the top so the drum can pass through.

Since the same setup will work for other rotary tools, it seemed logical to provide table inserts of different sizes. So the idea progressed to where drum sanding was just one of dozens of standard operations and advanced techniques that are accomplished more easily and accurately because of the jig. In fact, with the jig, you can do quite a few jobs that would be difficult to do otherwise, or that at least would require some special setup.

It's easy to set up the jig. The U-shaped slot at the rear of the table snugs around the drill press column, and the clamp ledge at the bottom of the case butts against the front of the

drill press table. This makes alignment automatic. The jig is secured by tightening a single C-clamp over the clamp ledge and the front of the table.

My master jig is sized for a Delta 7½" drill press with an 11" × 14" table, but alignment of the jig and its attachment method does not depend on the size of the tool's table. So, the sizes of components in the materials list should be generally applicable. However, you may have to design the slot and position the clamp ledge to suit your machine.

MAKING THE JIG

STEP 1: PREPARE THE TABLE

Cut the table to size and mark an accurate centerline across its width. Shape the slot by first forming an end-hole with a fly cutter or hole saw and then sawing away the waste on a scroll saw or band saw. It's essential that the slot be aligned precisely on the centerline. Put the table in place snug against the column, and use the drill press to drill a small hole on the centerline. This establishes the capacity of the machine—that is, the distance from the column to the center of the quill.

Carefully mark the locations of $\frac{5}{16}''$ threaded inserts at the top left corner of the table (for the pivoting fence), the two 3/8″ inserts for the shaper fence, and the two $\frac{3}{8}''$ inserts that will be used for fulcrum pins.

Drill the holes for the inserts and install them from the bottom of the table until they are almost flush with the table's surface.

Using the small hole in the table as a center point, work with a fly cutter or hole saw to form a $2\frac{3}{4}''$ diameter hole.

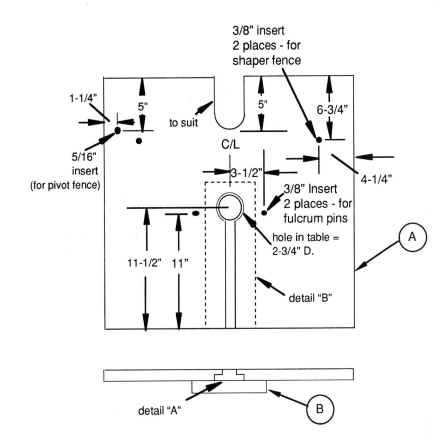

MATERIALS LIST				
DRILL PRESS MASTER JIG **Table**				
QTY.	KEY	NAME	SIZE (IN INCHES)	MATERIAL
1	A	Table	$\frac{3}{4} \times 24 \times 26$	Plywood
1	B	Support	$\frac{3}{4} \times 5 \times 14$	Plywood
$\frac{5}{16}''$ Threaded Insert (2)			No. $8 \times 1\frac{1}{4}''$ Flathead Screw (6)	
$\frac{3}{8}''$ Threaded Insert (4)			$\frac{5}{16}'' \times 1''$ Wing Bolt (1)	

STEP 2: FORM THE CENTERED T-SLOT (DETAIL "A")

Saw a 1"-wide opening down the center of the table, starting at the front of the table and ending at the hole. Enlarge the bottom half of the opening to 2"-wide. Do this by making repeat passes with a saw blade or use a dadoing tool. In either case, set the tool to cut ⅜"-deep. The result is a T-slot for "slides" that will be explained later.

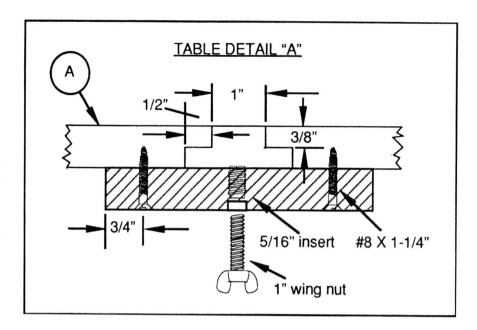

TABLE DETAIL "A"

A

1/2" 1" 3/8"

3/4"

5/16" insert   #8 X 1-1/4"

1" wing nut

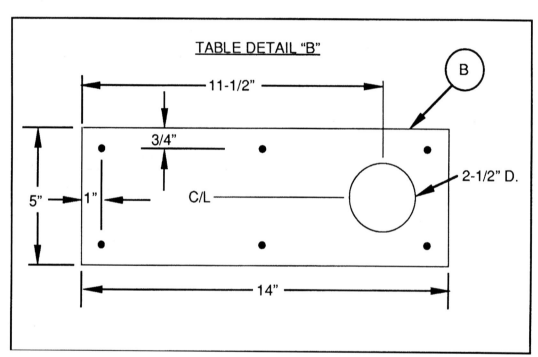

TABLE DETAIL "B"

B

11-1/2"

3/4"

5" 1" C/L

2-1/2" D.

14"

STEP 3: PROVIDE THE SUPPORT (DETAIL "B")

Cut the part to size and then, on its centerline, use a fly cutter or hole saw to form the 2½" diameter hole. Drill for and install the 5⁄16" threaded insert for the wing bolt that is used to secure the slides. Attach the support to the bottom of the table with six no. 8 × 1¼" flathead screws. Be sure the support is centered on the table and that its hole is concentric with the hole in the table.

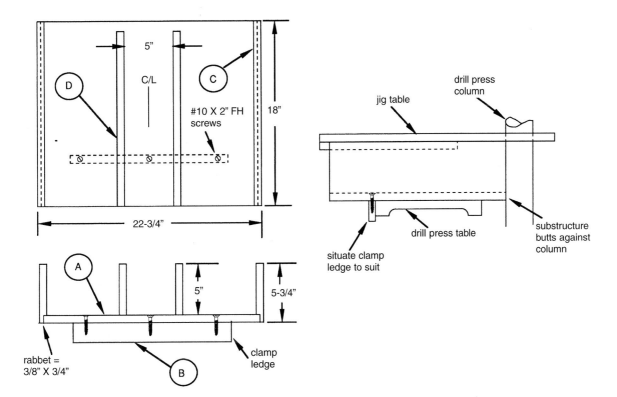

STEP 4: ASSEMBLE THE SUBSTRUCTURE

Cut the base (A) to size and mark a centerline across its width. Place the base on the drill press table so a bit in the machine's chuck will be on the marked centerline. Adjust the base so it butts against the column and its front edge is parallel with the table edge. Mark the location of the clamp ledge (B) and attach it to the base with glue and three no. 10×2″ flathead screws.

Prepare the sides (C) and the partitions (D) and then form a ⅜″-wide ×¾″-deep rabbet along one edge of the sides. Attach the sides to the base with glue and 4d finishing nails. Carefully mark the location of the partitions. They must be centered on the base with a 5″ space between them so their top edges will butt against the

support that is part of the jig's table. Coat the bottom edges of the partitions with glue, and secure them with clamps while you drive 6d finishing nails up through the base.

Coat the top edges of the partitions and sides with glue and put the table in place, holding it with clamps until the glue sets or use 6d finishing

nails to secure the connection. If so, set the nails and fill the holes with wood dough.

MATERIALS LIST				
DRILL PRESS MASTER JIG **Substructure**				
QTY.	KEY	NAME	SIZE (IN INCHES)	MATERIAL
1	A	Base	¾×18×22	Plywood
1	B	Clamp Ledge	¾×2×16	Hardwood
2	C	Sides	¾×5¾×18	Plywood
2	D	Partition	¾×5×17	Plywood
No. 10×2″ Flathead Screw (3)			Glue and Various Finishing Nails	

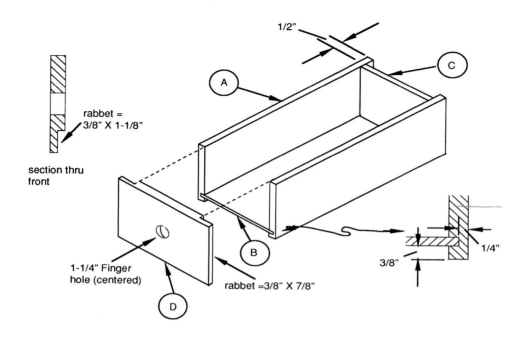

rabbet =
3/8" X 1-1/8"

section thru
front

1/2"

A

C

1-1/4" Finger
hole (centered)

D

B

rabbet =3/8" X 7/8"

1/4"

3/8"

MATERIALS LIST				
DRILL PRESS MASTER JIG				
Drawers				
QTY.	KEY	NAME	SIZE (IN INCHES)	MATERIAL
4	A	Sides	$\frac{1}{2} \times 4^{15}\!/_{16} \times 16$	Plywood
2	B	Bottom	$\frac{1}{4} \times 6\frac{7}{8} \times 16$	Plywood
2	C	Back	$\frac{3}{4} \times 4\frac{1}{4} \times 6\frac{3}{8}$	Softwood
2	D	Front	$\frac{3}{4} \times 5\frac{1}{2} \times 8$	Plywood
Glue and Various Finishing Nails				

STEP 5: MAKE THE DRAWERS

The drawers are not fancy, but suitable for the purpose. You might want to check to be sure the width and height allows the drawers to move smoothly in the jig.

Make the sides, and after cutting the ¼"-wide groove along the bottom edge, use glue to install the bottom. Add the back, securing it with glue and 4d finishing nails.

Cut the front to size and after boring the 1¼" finger hole, form the side and bottom rabbets so the part will fit nicely against the sides and bottom of the drawer. Attach the front with glue and 4d finishing nails, setting the nails and filling the holes with wood dough.

I used a finger hole instead of a drawer pull to avoid having anything project beyond the front of the jig.

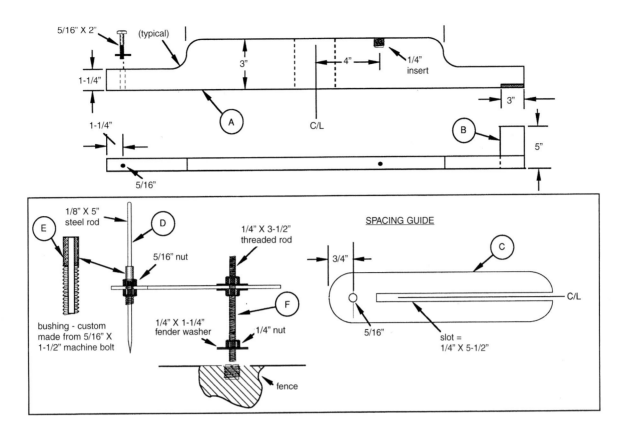

ADDING FENCES AND OTHER ACCESSORIES

STEP 6: PIVOTING FENCE

Cut the part (A) to size and mark a centerline across its width. Saw the part to its profile shape on a scroll saw or band saw and smooth the sawed edges with a drum sander.

Drill the hole for $\frac{5}{16}'' \times 2''$ bolt at the inboard end and then the hole for the $\frac{1}{4}''$ threaded insert. The hole for the insert can be deeper than necessary, but install the insert so it will be flush with the top edge of the fence.

Make repeat passes with a saw blade or use a dadoing tool to form the $\frac{1}{4}''$-deep $\times 3''$-wide notch at the outboard end of the fence, and then install the clamp ledge (B) with glue and a few small brads.

STEP 7: PREPARE THE SPACING GUIDE

The spacing guide is used on the pivoting fence to automatically establish the distance between equally spaced holes that are needed on a common centerline.

Start by forming the guide bar (C) from a 7" length of $1\frac{1}{2}''$-wide aluminum bar stock. Round off each end and then drill the $\frac{5}{16}''$ attachment hole and a $\frac{1}{4}''$ end-hole for the slot. Clean out the waste on a scroll saw or band saw and smooth the sawed edges with a file.

Next, make the bushing (E) by removing the head of a $\frac{5}{16}'' \times 1\frac{1}{2}''$ machine bolt and drilling a $\frac{1}{8}''$ hole

MATERIALS LIST				
DRILL PRESS MASTER JIG				
Pivot Fence				
QTY.	KEY	NAME	SIZE (IN INCHES)	MATERIAL
1	A	Fence	$1\frac{1}{2} \times 3 \times 26$	Hardwood
1	B	Clamp Ledge	$\frac{1}{4} \times 3 \times 5$	Plywood
1	C	Guide Bar	$\frac{1}{8} \times 1\frac{1}{2} \times 7$	Aluminum
1	D	Guide Post	$\frac{1}{8} \times 5$	Steel Rod
1	E	Bushing	$\frac{5}{16} \times 1\frac{1}{2}$	Machine Bolt
1	F	Riser Rod	$\frac{1}{4} \times 3\frac{1}{2}$	Thread Rod

$\frac{1}{4}''$ Threaded Insert (1) $\frac{5}{16}''$ Nut (2)

$\frac{5}{16}'' \times 2''$ Bolt (1) $\frac{1}{4}'' \times 1\frac{1}{4}''$ Fender Washer (4)

$\frac{1}{4}''$ Nut (3)

Secure the pivoting fence with a small C-clamp. Distance between the bit and the fence determines edge distance. The spacing guide is adjusted to automatically judge the distance between a series of holes.

Straight routing with the pivoting fence guiding the work. Note the use of the special chuck—called "spindle adapter" or "holding collet chuck" by manufacturers—that is used in place of the regular chuck to minimize the effect of side-thrust. Make repeat passes to achieve full depth-of-cut when necessary. Use the machine's highest speed; feed slowly from left-to-right. (The guard is not shown in all the photos.)

concentrically through it. Do this by gripping the bolt perpendicularly in a drill press vise and drilling a $\frac{1}{16}$" pilot hole. Then enlarge the hole to $\frac{1}{8}$". Secure the bushing in the bar with two $\frac{5}{16}$" nuts.

The riser rod (F) that threads into the insert that is in the fence is a length of $\frac{1}{4}$" threaded stock. The $\frac{1}{4}$" nut at the bottom locks the rod in place: The two top nuts are used to adjust the height of the guide bar. The guide post (D) is a 5" length of $\frac{1}{8}$" steel rod, pointed at one end. In use, the spacing guide is used to drill pilot holes that are later enlarged to the needed size.

STEP 8: MAKE A SHAPER FENCE

Before going further, let's consider the thought that since 3-lip shaper cutters (and router bits) are, essentially, side cutters, using them in a drill press might damage the tool's drilling accuracy. Actually, modern quality drill presses are designed with heavy-duty ball bearings that can stand up to radial loads.

Speed is another factor. We know that shapers and routers rotate at rpms much greater than what is available on a drill press. The answer is to move the work more slowly than you would on a machine that is designed for the applications. A slower feed lets the cutter pass over a given area of the work a greater number of times, thus compensating for fewer rpms.

Depth-of-cut is a negligible factor. Achieving very deep cuts by making repeat passes is recommended practice that applies to drill press shaping and routing as well as to other tools.

Begin construction of the shaper fence by preparing the base (A) and the clamp bar (B). Drill the $\frac{7}{16}$" hole

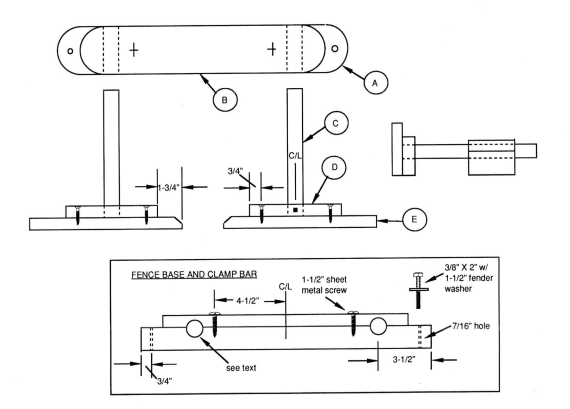

FENCE BASE AND CLAMP BAR

4-1/2"

1-1/2" sheet metal screw

3/8" X 2" w/ 1-1/2" fender washer

7/16" hole

3-1/2"

see text

3/4"

C/L

at each end of the base for the ⅜" bolts that will thread into the inserts that are in the jig's table. The holes are larger than needed to provide for slight adjustments when the fence is used.

Clamp the parts together and mark the location of the holes for the posts (C). The steel tubes have a ¹⁷⁄₁₆" outside diameter so if you supply the same-size hole and then reduce the thickness of the clamp bar a bit by sanding, the bar will bear down on the tubes enough to hold them securely. Drill pilot holes for the sheet metal screws while the parts are clamped together.

Cut the parts needed for the backups (D) and the fences (E) to size. Drill a ⅞" hole through the backups for the post and then use a suitably sized drum sander or work with a round file to enlarge the hole just enough to provide a tight fit for the posts. Coat the end of the posts with an epoxy before tapping them into place. Reinforce the connection by

drilling a pilot hole through the top edge of the backup on the centerline of the post, and then installing a 1"-long sheet metal screw.

The fences must rest on the table when the unit is used. To be sure of this, mark their location while the

base is locked to the jig's table and the clamp bar is gripping the posts. Coat the face of the backups with glue and hold the fences in position with small clamps. Install the no. 10 × 1¼" flathead screws from the rear surface of the backups.

MATERIALS LIST				
DRILL PRESS MASTER JIG				
Shaper Fence				
QTY.	KEY	NAME	SIZE (IN INCHES)	MATERIAL
1	A	Base	1½ × 3 × 19	Hardwood
1	B	Clamp Bar	¾ × 3 × 16	Hardwood
2	C	Posts	(See Text)	Steel Tube
2	D	Backup	¾ × 2½ × 6	Hardwood
2	E	Fence	¾ × 3¼ × 10	Hardwood Or Hardboard Faced Plywood

⅜" × 2" Machine Bolt (2)

⅜" × 1¼" Fender Washer (2)

1½" Sheet Metal Screw (2)

⅞" Sheet Metal Screw (4)

No. 10 × 1¼" Flathead Screw (8)

Working with the shaper fence. Here, a rabbeting bit, which is normally used in a portable router, is held by the special chuck. Position the fences to gauge the width of the cut. Move the work from left-to-right.

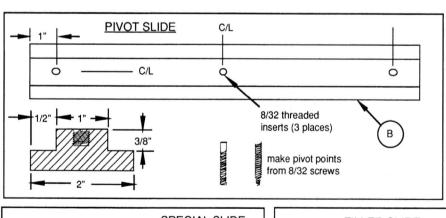

PIVOT SLIDE

1" C/L

C/L

8/32 threaded inserts (3 places)

B

1/2" 1"

3/8"

2"

make pivot points from 8/32 screws

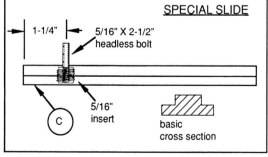

SPECIAL SLIDE

1-1/4" 5/16" X 2-1/2" headless bolt

C

5/16" insert

basic cross section

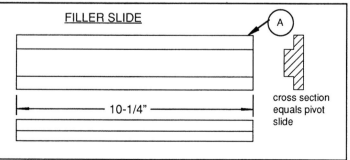

FILLER SLIDE

A

10-1/4"

cross section equals pivot slide

Use the pivot slide when holes are needed on a circular path. Impale the work on the pointed pivot pin when the work does not require a center hole.

STEP 9: MAKE THE SLIDES

Several types of slides are needed, but they all have the same cross-section shape and dimensions. Cut a ¾″ × 2″ strip of wood about 36″-long, and then work with a dadoing tool to provide a ⅜″-deep × ½″-wide rabbet along each edge.

Cut off a piece 15″-long for the pivot slide (B) and install the three 8/32 threaded inserts on its centerline. Make the pivot points from 8/32 screws. The pointed one is used when the work does not have a center hole.

Cut off a 10″-long piece from the parent stock for the special slide (C) and install the ⁵⁄₁₆″ threaded insert. We'll talk later about the several functions this slide is used for.

The last slide (A), 10¼″ long, is just a filler, used to close the gap in the jig's table when other slides are not being used.

MATERIALS LIST				
DRILL PRESS MASTER JIG				
Slides				
QTY.	KEY	NAME	SIZE (IN INCHES)	MATERIAL
1	A	Filler	¾ × 2 × 10¼	Hardwood
1	B	Pivot	¾ × 2 × 15	Hardwood
1	C	Special	¾ × 2 × 10	Hardwood
8/32 Threaded Insert (3)			⁵⁄₁₆″ Threaded Insert (1)	
8/32 × 1″ Screw for Pivot Point (2)			⁵⁄₁₆″ × 2½″ Bolt (1)	

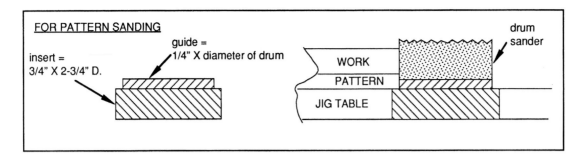

FOR PATTERN SANDING

insert =
3/4" X 2-3/4" D.

guide =
1/4" X diameter of drum

WORK

PATTERN

JIG TABLE

drum
sander

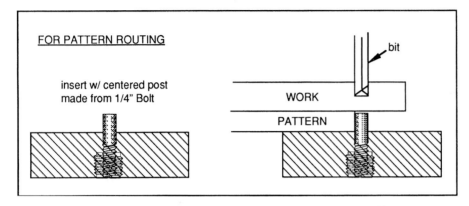

FOR PATTERN ROUTING

insert w/ centered post
made from 1/4" Bolt

WORK

PATTERN

bit

inserts w/ centered holes
to accommodate various
size drum sanders

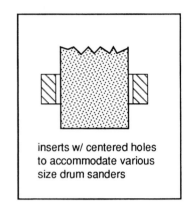

Drum sanding—the hole through the table allows full use of the abrasive area. Move the work against the drum's direction of rotation. A hose from a vacuum cleaner, placed in the opening between the drawers, will collect much of the saw dust.

STEP 10: SUPPLY THE INSERTS

All inserts have a 2¾″ diameter and are ¾″ thick. The inserts serve various functions. For example—one with a top centered guide with a diameter to match that of the sanding drum to be used—is installed for pattern sanding.

For pattern routing, the disc has a centered threaded insert to receive a short stud.

Other inserts for simple drum sanding have central holes that suit the diameter of the sander being used.

Work with a fly cutter or hole saw to produce several of the inserts. Then, when needed, they can be finalized to suit a particular chore.

MATERIALS LIST
DRILL PRESS MASTER JIG
Inserts
All Inserts Are ¾″ × 2¾″ Hardwood—See Drawing and Text for Various Applications

"Jointing" with a drum sander. Take light cuts and keep the work moving. The drum will indent the edge of the workpiece if you stop the feed at any point.

Using the pivot slide for sanding the edge on circular components. Lock the pivot guide after positioning the work for light contact with the drum. Rotate the work clockwise. Sanding is for smoothing, not shaping, so don't try to remove a lot of material with a single pass.

Use the special slide to form grooves parallel to a curved edge. Turn the work to suit the curve: Use the pin as a fulcrum. Move the work slowly from right-to-left. The same setup can be used with a drum sander to smooth curved edges.

Use the pivot slide to guide the work for circular grooving. Rotate the work in a clockwise direction. The arrow indicates the pivot point.

Freehand shaping, required on curved edges, is done with one or both of the fulcrum pins in place. Here, a router bit with a ball bearing pilot is being used. Start by bracing the work against the "infeed" pin and then advancing the work slowly to make firm contact with the bearing. On some curved edges, it's a good idea to use the second fulcrum pin to support the work at the end of the cut.

STEP 11: PROVIDE A V-BLOCK

The V-block is a pretty straightforward chore, but be careful when attaching the block to the insert (B). Correct positioning at this point will assure accurate drilling later on. A good way to assemble: Put a small piece of carpet tape on the surface of the disc and then set the disc in the jig's table. Position the V-block so it lines up properly with a small bit in the drill press chuck and press it down on the tape. Remove the parts from the jig and, after marking the position of the disc, remove the tape and attach the disc permanently with glue.

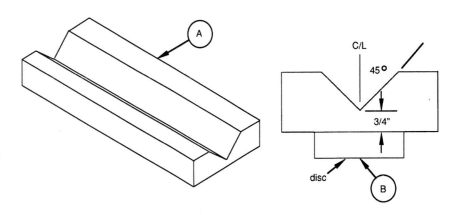

Accurate diametrical holes through tubing, rods or wood rounds, are easy to drill by using the V-block. You can also use the setup to drill into the corners of square stock, but start the hole carefully so the bit doesn't wander off the point. Tack-nail a slim strip of wood across the V to serve as a stop when the hole is required in several pieces of stock.

MATERIALS LIST				
DRILL PRESS MASTER JIG				
V-Block				
QTY.	KEY	NAME	SIZE (IN INCHES)	MATERIAL
1	A	Block	1½ × 4¾ × 12	Softwood
1	B	Base	(Use Insert)	Hardwood

Shaping can be done with 3-lip shaper cutters, but you need a special arbor or adapter in order to mount the cutters. Position the fences in relation to whether the cutter will make a full or partial cut. The arrow indicates feed-direction. Note the use of the guard.

QTY.	KEY	NAME	SIZE (IN INCHES)	MATERIAL
MATERIALS LIST				
DRILL PRESS MASTER JIG **Guard**				
1	A	Bracket	¾ × 2¾ × 4½	Hardwood
1	B	Shield	⅛ × 7 × 7	Lexan
8/32 Threaded Insert (2)			8/32 × ⅝″ Round Head Screw with Washer (2)	
¼″ × 2¾″ Bolt with Nut and Lock Washer (1)				

STEP 12: MAKE A GUARD

Drill presses are not equipped with guards. For most operations you can operate safely by obeying the basic safety rules—clamp workpieces and judge the best position for your hands. But for chores like routing and shaping that require both hands to control and move the stock, a safety shield makes sense.

The one I made for use with the master jig mounts on a U-shaped bracket (A) that is attached to my Delta drill press with a bolt that substitutes for the one used to secure the split casting that supports the depth-stop rod. Check your machine to see if customizing of the bracket is necessary.

Prepare the bracket by making the layout shown in the drawing. Install the two 8/32 threaded inserts and drill the four corner holes. Remove

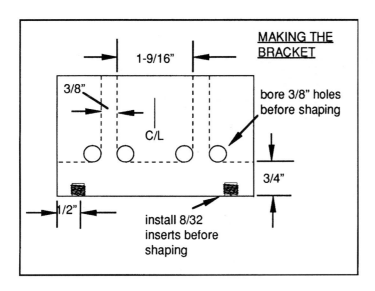

MAKING THE BRACKET

1-9/16"

3/8"

C/L

bore 3/8" holes before shaping

3/4"

1/2"

install 8/32 inserts before shaping

the waste by sawing on a scroll saw or band saw, then bore the attachment holes with the bracket resting vertically on a block of wood.

Form the slots in the shield in the usual recommended fashion. That is, drill end-holes and clean out the waste by sawing. I used Lexan for the shield, but any clear rigid plastic will do.

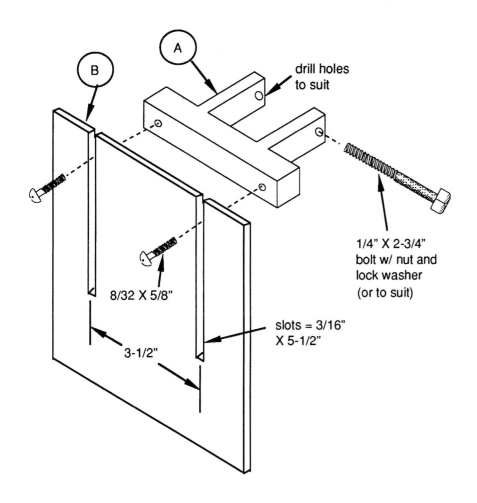

A

B

drill holes to suit

1/4" X 2-3/4" bolt w/ nut and lock washer (or to suit)

8/32 X 5/8"

3-1/2"

slots = 3/16" X 5-1/2"

Band Saw Overarm Pivot Jig

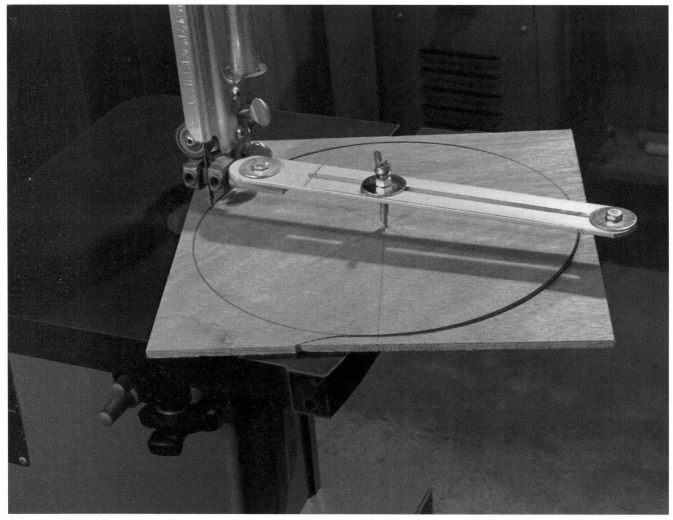

The height of the jig is controlled by the machine's guide post. Since the guard is part of the post/blade-guide assembly, it will always be positioned for safe operation. Use a sharp blade with uniform set.

An adjustable pivot-type jig provides for controlled sawing of perfect circular components. It's especially useful when several similar parts are needed. A pivot point can be just a nail driven through a board that is clamped to the table, but that's a chancy setup. Making a jig that is easy to install when needed and that can be retained as a permanent accessory for the band saw is a more professional approach.

The overarm pivot jig in my shop has several advantages: The overhead pivot point is easy to locate on the work, and the arm can be adjusted left or right to be sure the pivot point is directly in line with the saw blade's teeth. Also, some adjustment can be made to compensate for any "lead" the blade might have.

The pivot jig can be used to saw elliptical shapes. Mark center points on a common centerline and then make two cuts, each using a different pivot location. The arrow indicates the pivot point that was used for the first cut.

Use the pivot jig to produce similar arc-shaped components. Set up by establishing a series of equally spaced pivot points on a common centerline. This is also the way to round off one or both ends of a workpiece.

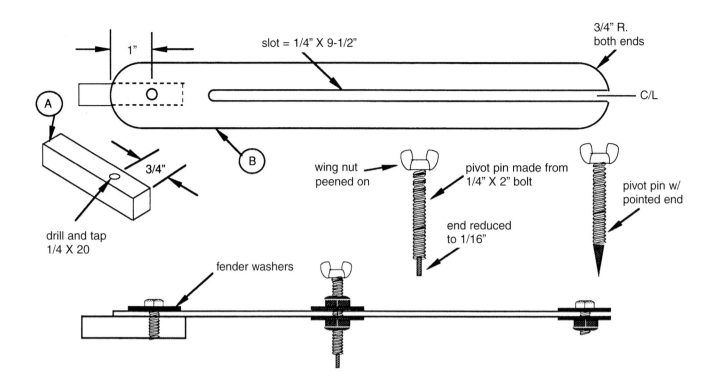

1"

slot = 1/4" X 9-1/2"

3/4" R.
both ends

C/L

A

3/4"

B

drill and tap
1/4 X 20

wing nut
peened on

pivot pin made from
1/4" X 2" bolt

pivot pin w/
pointed end

end reduced
to 1/16"

fender washers

		MATERIALS LIST		
		BAND SAW PIVOT JIG		
QTY.	KEY	NAME	SIZE (IN INCHES)	MATERIAL
1	A	Arm Mount	1/2 × 1/2 × 2 1/2	Steel Bar
1	B	Arm	1/8 × 1 1/2 × 12	Aluminum
1/4-20 × 5/8" Bolt (1)			1/4-20 Nut (4)	
1/4-20 × 1/2" Bolt (1)			1/4-20 × 2" Bolt (1)	
1/4" × 1 1/4" Fender Washer (5)			1/4-20 Wing Nut (1)	

MAKING THE JIG

STEP 1: MAKE THE ARM

Provide a 12″ length of 1/8″ × 1 1/2″ aluminum strap (available at large hardware stores), and round off both ends. Drill the 1/4″ attachment hole and a 1/4″ end-hole for the slot. Complete the slot by sawing on the band saw or a scroll saw. Smooth the sawed edges with a file.

STEP 2: MAKE THE ARM MOUNT

The arm mount is a piece of steel bar stock (often called "keyway stock") whose cross-section dimensions—in my case, 1/2″ × 1/2″—equal those of the right-hand blade guide that it will replace when the jig is used. Smooth and square the ends of the bar stock with a fine file.

Mark the location of the hole in the arm mount with a center punch and, while gripping the part in a drill-press vise, drill the hole (in stages) and tap it for a 1/4-20 bolt.

STEP 3: MAKE THE PIVOT PINS

Use a hacksaw to remove the heads from a pair of $\frac{1}{4}'' \times 2''$ bolts. Chuck the bolts in a drill press and use a file to reduce the end of one to $\frac{1}{16}''$ and to form a point on the end of the other one. Shaping the end of the bolts can also be done by gripping the headless bolts in a portable drill and spinning them against a turning grinding wheel. Work slowly, have the grinder's shield in place, and, as always, wear safety goggles.

Complete the pin design by placing a wing nut at the top end and securing it by indenting with a prick punch.

STEP 4: ADD THE HARDWARE

Close the open end of the slot by using top and bottom fender washers and the $\frac{1}{2}''$-long bolt. Install the pivot pin with top and bottom fender washers and nuts. The pins are adjustable vertically and can be secured at any point along the slot.

Attach the arm to the arm mount with a fender washer and the $\frac{5}{8}''$-long bolt. Install the jig in place of the band saw's right-hand blade guide (see drawing at top right).

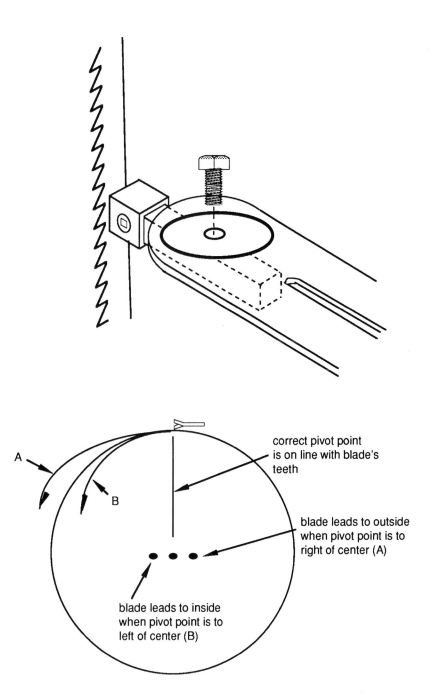

correct pivot point is on line with blade's teeth

blade leads to outside when pivot point is to right of center (A)

blade leads to inside when pivot point is to left of center (B)

USING THE JIG

In order to get perfect circular cuts, the pivot point must be in line with the points on the blade's teeth. If the pivot point is to the left, the blade will track to the inside of the work. Conversely, the blade will track to the outside of the work when the pivot point is to the right of center (see drawing at bottom right).

There are two ways to operate: Prepare the work a bit oversize and make a freehand cut to the line be-

fore securing the pivot pin. This permits an uninterrupted circular cut. Or, start with a square piece with sides equal to the diameter of the circle, and start cutting with the work butted against the saw blade. The second idea saves material, but is a little chancy, since the blade will have to enter the work in four places; a factor that can lead to blemishes.

Controlled sawing can be used to produce several similar pieces in one operation. Make a pad of the number of pieces required by tack-nailing or with carpet tape, and then saw the pad as you would a solid piece.

Band Saw Master Jig

The oversize table of the master jig is an asset to any home workshop band saw. Homegrown fence and a miter gauge add new dimensions to the tool. I sized the groove in the table for an on-hand miter gauge. The new table has limited tilt action, but it's easy to remove should you need bevel cuts that are beyond its capacity.

I f you use the band saw merely for freehand sawing of curved components and an occasional resaw chore, you're selling short what actually is one of the most versatile wood-cutting machines. Just adding an oversize table is a plus factor for a home-shop band saw since its work support area isn't very generous. But when you supply accessories for splitting plain cylinders or turnings, sawing parallel curves, pattern sawing, controlled circular sawing, crosscutting round stock plus other practical add-ons, the band saw is elevated to the status it deserves (see examples on page 69).

The Master Jig in my shop was designed for an average "small" machine. If your unit is in the 12″ to 14″ size range with a table that measures in the 12″ to 14″-square area, you should be able to duplicate the jig without much fuss. Some customizing may be needed, so I'll point up critical areas as we go.

Check two fundamental alignment

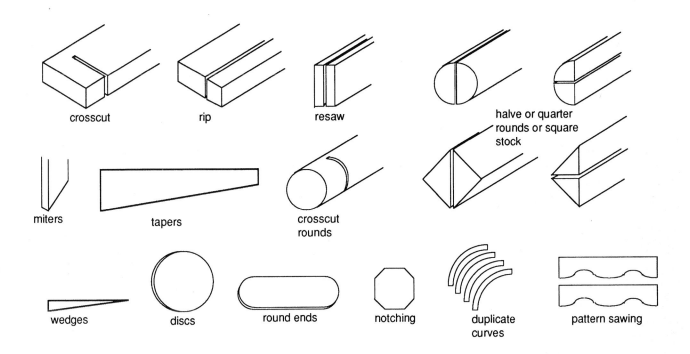

crosscut

rip

resaw

halve or quarter rounds or square stock

miters

tapers

crosscut rounds

wedges

discs

round ends

notching

duplicate curves

pattern sawing

factors before starting construction. The vertical angle between the saw blade and the table, with the trunnion set at zero, must be 90°. The side of the saw blade and the miter-gauge slot must be parallel.

MATERIALS LIST				
BAND SAW MASTER JIG				
Table				
QTY.	KEY	NAME	SIZE (IN INCHES)	MATERIAL
1	A	Table	¾ × 24 × 26	Plywood
1	B	Table Guide	⅜ × ¾ × 24	Hardwood
1	C	Brace	¾ × 4 × 7	Plywood
2	D	Table Lock	1½ × 1¼ × 1¼	Aluminum Angle
1	E	Table Tie	⅛ × 1½ × 4	Aluminum
1	F	Fence Brace	¾ × 1½ × 13½	Hardwood

5/16″ Threaded Insert (3)   ¼″ × 1″ Thumb Screw (1)

¼″ Threaded Insert (1)   ⅝″ Round Head Screw (4)

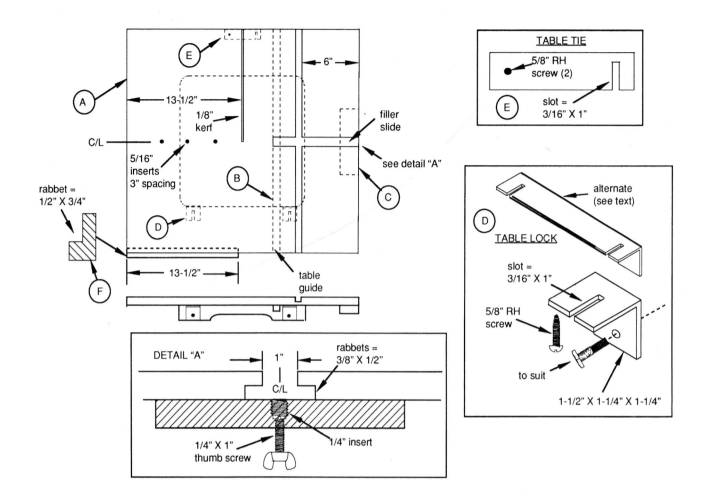

TABLE TIE

5/8" RH screw (2)

slot = 3/16" X 1"

E

DETAIL "A"

1"

C/L

rabbets = 3/8" X 1/2"

1/4" X 1" thumb screw

1/4" insert

TABLE LOCK

alternate (see text)

slot = 3/16" X 1"

5/8" RH screw

to suit

1-1/2" X 1-1/4" X 1-1/4"

D

E

6"

13-1/2"

1/8" kerf

filler slide

see detail "A"

C/L

5/16" inserts 3" spacing

B

C

rabbet = 1/2" X 3/4"

13-1/2"

table guide

F

A

D

MAKING THE JIG

STEP 1: START WITH THE TABLE

Prepare a piece of cabinet-grade plywood for the table and then work on a table saw to form the ⅛" kerf. The center of the 1"-wide × 9"-long slot that is needed for filler and pivot slides (shown later) is aligned with the center of the table. Work on the table saw to make outline cuts that are shorter than needed, and then extend the cuts with a handsaw. Remove the waste with a chisel. Alternately, if the tool's capacity permits it, form the slot by working on the band saw.

Next, widen the bottom half of the slot to 2" (see detail [A] above) with a dadoing tool or by making repeat passes with a saw blade. The cuts are actually rabbets that are ⅜"-deep × ½"-wide.

Use a dadoing tool to form the slot that is needed for a miter gauge. Locate it 6" away from the right edge of the table, and size its depth and width to suit the bar of an on-hand miter gauge. Drill holes for the three ⁵⁄₁₆" threaded inserts, and install them through the bottom of the table until they are almost flush with the table's surface.

STEP 2: ADD THE TABLE GUIDE

Size the table guide (B) so it will slide smoothly in the machine's table slot. Put the guide in place and add the jig's table so its right edge and the guide are parallel. Secure the position of the guide by tack-nailing through the table. Attach the guide permanently with glue and four no. 4 × ¾" flathead screws, installing the screws from the bottom of the guide. Drill adequate shank and pilot holes for the screws so they won't spread the bar when they are installed.

STEP 3: ADD FENCE AND TABLE BRACES

Prepare the part for the fence brace (F), and then use a dadoing tool to form the ½" × ¾" rabbet. This is a slim piece, so use a pusher to move it past the cutter. Attach the brace to the table with glue and 4d finishing nails.

You can do accurate crosscutting with a miter gauge as long as the saw blade is sharp and its teeth have even set. Steady feed without forcing the blade leads to quality work. The generous table provides good support for workpieces.

Cut the table brace (C) to size and install the ¼″ threaded insert (see detail [A] on page 70). Coat contact areas of brace and table with glue, and use a pair of clamps to keep the brace in place until the glue sets.

STEP 4: ADD THE TABLE LOCKS AND TIE

Use aluminum angle with 1¼″ legs for the table locks (D). If ready-made angle isn't available, make your own from aluminum strap. A single piece of aluminum angle can be be used instead of a pair of locks. The slot in the top leg of the angle is needed so the jig's table can be moved to-and-fro. Why? Because some pivot-guided work that can be done with the new table requires good alignment between blade teeth and pivot point. Allowing for adjustment to assure this, regardless of blade width (and tracking), is necessary for accurate sawing.

Drill holes through the vertical leg of the locks to match the holes that are in the drill press table for adding after-market accessories like fence rails. Use suitable bolts to secure the locks to the drill press table and put the jig's table in place. Use an awl to pierce the underside of the table at the *front end* of the slot in the lock and then install the ⅜″ round head screws.

Make the table tie (E) from aluminum strap and attach it to the underside of the table so it spans the ⅛″ kerf. The purpose of the tie is to maintain the table's levelness on both sides of the kerf.

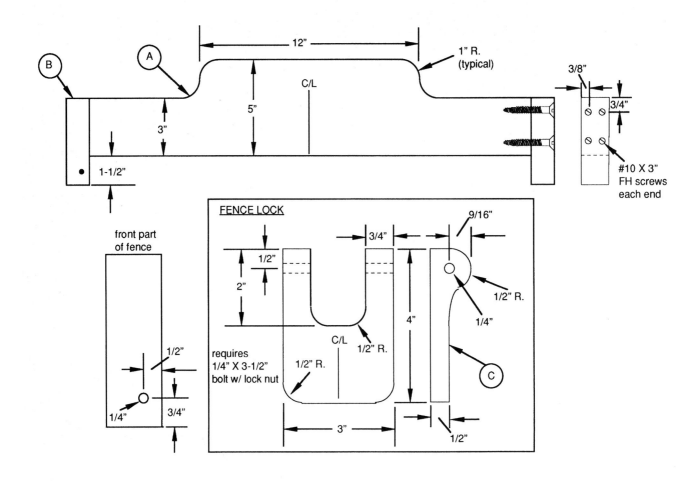

MATERIALS LIST				
BAND SAW MASTER JIG				
Fence				
QTY.	KEY	NAME	SIZE (IN INCHES)	MATERIAL
1	A	Body	1½ × 5 × 24¼	Hardwood
2	B	Ends	1¼ × 1½ × 4½	Hardwood
1	C	Table Lock	1 × 3 × 4¼	Hardwood
No. 10 × 3″ Flathead Screw (8)			¼″ × 3½″ Bolt with Lock Nut (1)	

ADDING ACCESSORIES
PROVIDE A FENCE

STEP 1: PREPARE THE BODY

Cut stock for the body (A) to overall size and shape the top edge on the band saw. Use a drum sander to smooth the sawed edge.

STEP 2: ADD THE END PARTS

Cut the ends (B) to size and install the rear one with glue and four no. 10 × 3″ flathead screws. Be sure to drill adequate shank and body holes and to countersink carefully before driving the screws. Before installing

Ripping on the band saw is a good way to size work to width. As always, a sharp blade with even set does the best job. Use a push stick instead of your hands to move narrow work past the blade. Note the filler slide in the table. The only time you need to remove it is when using the pivot slide for circular sawing.

the front end-piece, carefully locate and drill the hole that is needed for the fence lock.

STEP 3: MAKE THE LOCK

Cut the part (C) to size and accurately locate and drill the ¼" hole. Lay out the shape of the centered opening and saw away the waste on a scroll saw or the band saw. Use the band saw to shape the lock's edge-profile, but don't try to shape the rounded end exactly at this point. Instead, work by hand with sandpaper to "dress" the end so that, when the lock is pivoted downward, the rounded end will bear firmly against the fence brace to secure the fence's position.

Keep the fence lock horizontal to place or remove the fence. Pivot it downward to lock the fence. The bearing edge of the lock is hand-tailored so it will provide adequate pressure against the fence brace.

PROVIDE THE SLIDES

The filler slide (A) and the pivot slide (B) have the same cross-section shape and dimensions, so a good procedure is to start with parent stock that is approximately 25″ long, and cut pieces to length after rabbeting the edges of the material. Do the rabbeting with a dado tool; use a push stick to move the work past the cutter. See the drawing at the top of page 76.

When the filler slide is in place, you'll see that it runs across the miter gauge groove in the jig's table. So, mark the location of the groove on the slide and then notch it so it won't interfere with using a miter gauge.

Mark the locations of the three 8/32 threaded inserts that are needed in the pivot slide. Drill for and install the inserts so they will be flush with the top surface of the slide.

Make the pivot points by removing the head from 8/32 screws. Chuck one of them in a drill press and form a point with a file, or, grip the screw in a portable drill and spin it against a turning grinding wheel.

The high section of the fence provides support for resawing chores. Results are best when the blade is in pristine condition. The thickness of the jig's table decreases depth-of-cut, but that's hardly critical on most band saws.

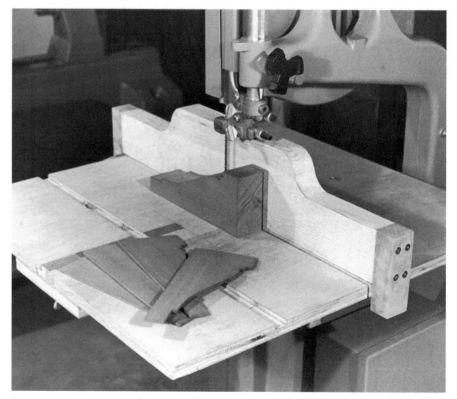

Resawing isn't just for reducing stock-thickness or transforming a thick board into several thin ones. If you preshape a component and then resaw, you can easily produce as many duplicate parts as you need.

The fence is adaptable for making taper cuts. You can use a commercial, adjustable taper jig if one is available, but there are other ways to go. (See next photo.)

You can do tapering (or form wedges) with a guide that rides the fence. Cut the shape that's needed, or the part that must be removed from the work, from a board or piece of plywood. Adjust the fence so the saw blade is at the edge of the guide. Place the work in the cutout in the guide and move both pieces past the blade.

A notching guide is a rectangular piece of wood with a particular shape cut into one edge. The cutout, V-shaped in this example, can be the shape of the part you need or what you wish to remove from the work. Keep the work snug in the cutout and move work and guide past the blade.

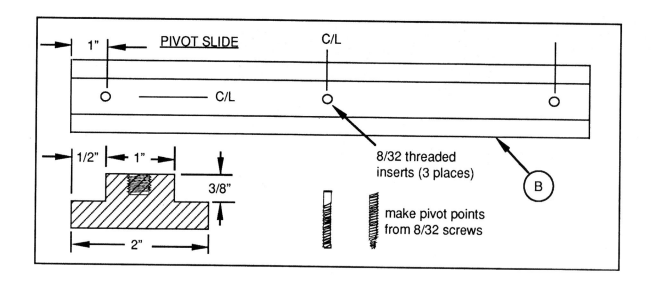

PIVOT SLIDE

8/32 threaded
inserts (3 places)

make pivot points
from 8/32 screws

B

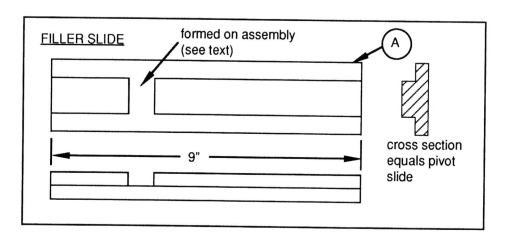

FILLER SLIDE

formed on assembly
(see text)

A

9"

cross section
equals pivot
slide

MATERIALS LIST				
BAND SAW MASTER JIG				
Slides				
QTY.	KEY	NAME	SIZE (IN INCHES)	MATERIAL
1	A	Filler	¾ × 2 × 9	Hardwood
1	B	Pivot Slide	¾ × 2 × 15	Hardwood
8/32 Threaded Insert (3)			8/32 Screws for Pivot Points	

ADD A PARALLEL V-BLOCK

STEP 1: MAKE THE BLOCK

Referring to the drawing on page 78, cut material for the block (B) to size and then form the V-shaped trough down its center.

STEP 2: ADD THE BASE AND GUIDE

Prepare the base (A) and attach it to the bottom of the block with glue and brads. Size the guide (C) so it will fit snugly in the table's miter gauge slot. A little on the tight side is good to prevent the accessory from moving when it is in use.

Put the guide in place in the table groove and then position the block/

base-assembly so the cut-path of the saw blade will be on the center of the V-cut. Mark the position of the guide and attach it to the underside of the base with glue and brads.

Place the accessory in position and, with a fine saw blade mounted, saw a kerf about 6"-long.

MAKE THE SPLITTER

Round off the top forward edge of the splitter (D) and use some emery paper to smooth the edge. The splitter should fit tightly in the kerf. If not, cover the bottom edge with plastic tape to thicken it a bit.

Use the pivot slide for controlled circular sawing. Lock the slide's position so the distance from the pivot point to the blade equals the radius of the circle. If you cut the work a bit oversize and make a free-hand cut to the line before impaling the work on the pivot pin, you can saw in one continuous pass. Adjust the table whenever necessary so the pivot point is aligned with the teeth on the blade. Keep the guard close to the work even though it's not shown so in all the photos.

Use the pivot slide to round off one or both ends of a component. The arrow indicates the first pivot point that was used to round off one end of the workpiece. The technique can also be used to shape arced pieces.

MATERIALS LIST				
BAND SAW MASTER JIG				
Parallel V-Block				
QTY.	KEY	NAME	SIZE (IN INCHES)	MATERIAL
1	A	Base	¼ × 10 × 11½	Plywood
1	B	Block	1⅞ × 4 × 11½	Hardwood
1	C	Guide	⅜ × ¾ × 16	Hardwood
1	D	Splitter	1⁄16 × 3 × 6	Aluminum

PARALLEL V-BLOCK

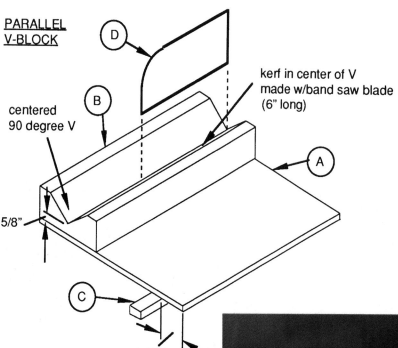

kerf in center of V
made w/band saw blade
(6" long)

centered
90 degree V

5/8"

1-1/2"

The parallel V-block makes it easy to saw rounds or turnings (or square stock) exactly in half. After the first pass, the parts can be sawed again to produce quarter-rounds. The splitter does the job of maintaining correct alignment. Use the jig to find centers on round or square stock that you plan to mount in a lathe.

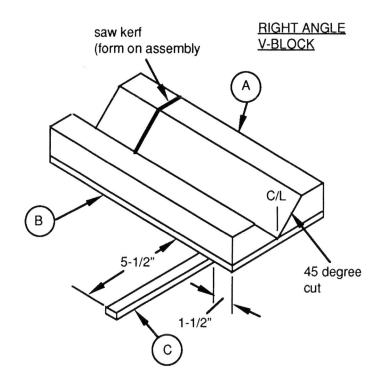

saw kerf
(form on assembly

A

B

C/L

5-1/2"

45 degree
cut

1-1/2"

C

ASSEMBLE THE RIGHT-ANGLE V-BLOCK

Parts (A) are similar, so prepare them by making a 45° bevel cut along one edge of 24"-long stock and halve the piece. Use glue and brads to attach the two pieces to the base (B) so they form a V-shaped trough.

Shape the guide (C) so it will ride smoothly in the table slot. Put the guide in the slot and position the V-assembly so the angle between its forward edge and the side of the saw is 90°. Mark the position of the guide and then attach it permanently to the block with glue and small nails.

Crosscutting round stock can be tricky because the blade tends to spin the work, but not so with the right angle V-block, because the work is held snugly in the V-trough. Also, the jig assures a square cut. Advance the jig only far enough for the kerf to span the V.

MATERIALS LIST			
BAND SAW MASTER JIG **Right Angle V-Block**			
QTY.	KEY	NAME	SIZE (IN INCHES)	MATERIAL
2	A	Block	1½ × 3 × 12	Hardwood
1	B	Base	¼ × 6 × 12	Plywood
1	C	Guide	⅜ × ¾ × 16	Hardwood

PARALLEL CURVES GUIDE

Shape the front end of the guide (A) on the band saw and smooth the sawed edges with a drum sander. Drill a 5/16″ end-hole for the slot and then saw out the waste. The guide is secured to the jig's table with 5/16″ bolts that thread into the inserts that were installed in the table.

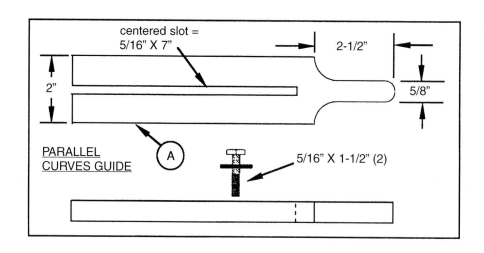

centered slot =
5/16" X 7"

2"

2-1/2"

5/8"

PARALLEL
CURVES GUIDE

A

5/16" X 1-1/2" (2)

Using the parallel curves guide. The first step is to shape the first edge freehand and sand it smooth. Set the guide point in line with the teeth on the saw blade and then secure the guide to gauge the width of the cut. The technique here is to keep the cut point and the guide point on the same line throughout the pass. The curve of the work is always tangent to the guide's control point.

		MATERIALS LIST		
		BAND SAW MASTER JIG		
		Parallel Curves Guide		
QTY.	KEY	NAME	SIZE (IN INCHES)	MATERIAL
1	A	Body	⅞ × 2 × 10	Hardwood

5/16″ × 1½″ Bolt with Washer (2)

PATTERN SAWING GUIDE

The pattern sawing guide (A) is shaped like the one made for parallel, curves, except that the slot is shorter and the business end is notched to fit the saw blade that is used. The riser (B) is needed so the guide will be elevated above the workpiece.

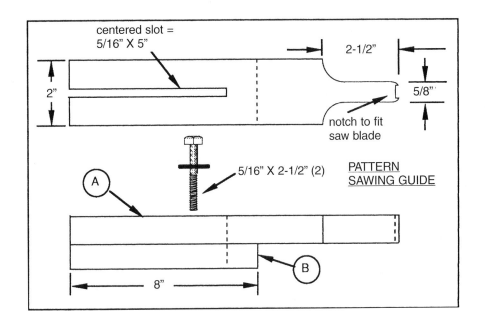

centered slot = 5/16" X 5"

2"

2-1/2"

5/8"

notch to fit saw blade

5/16" X 2-1/2" (2)

A

B

8"

PATTERN SAWING GUIDE

Using the pattern sawing guide. Lock the guide in place so the saw blade sits nicely in the notch that is in the end of the guide. Start by cutting a pattern that is the shape you need. Workpieces are cut to approximate size and attached to the bottom of the pattern by tack-nailing or with double-faced tape. As you move the pattern along the edge of the guide, the work is cut to the same shape. Move the work slowly and maintain contact between the pattern and the guide.

MATERIALS LIST				
BAND SAW MASTER JIG				
Pattern Sawing Guide				
QTY.	KEY	NAME	SIZE (IN INCHES)	MATERIAL
1	A	Body	$7/8 \times 2 \times 10\frac{1}{2}$	Hardwood
1	B	Riser	$7/8 \times 2 \times 6$	Hardwood
$5/16'' \times 2\frac{1}{2}''$ Bolt with Washer (2)				

Radial Arm Saw Horizontal Sawing Table 1

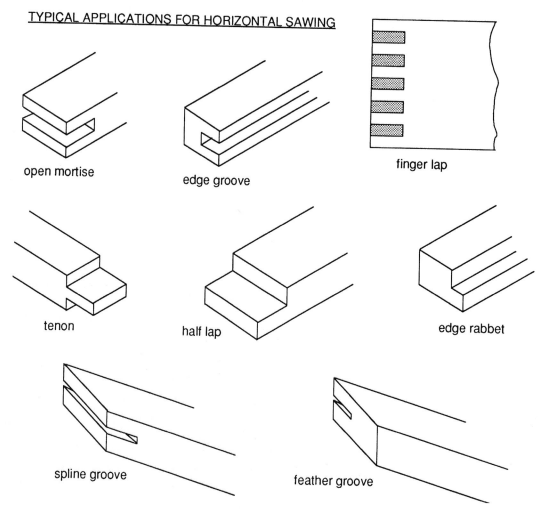

TYPICAL APPLICATIONS FOR HORIZONTAL SAWING

open mortise

edge groove

finger lap

tenon

half lap

edge rabbet

spline groove

feather groove

Horizontal sawing on the radial arm saw is possible because the motor can be tilted to a vertical position that situates the saw blade, or a dadoing tool, parallel to the table. The setup makes it possible to produce forms like those above that would be difficult to do otherwise. For some cuts the work is in a fixed position, and the motor is moved along the arm in normal fashion. Other times, the motor is locked in place and the work is moved for the cut.

Since the saw blade, when in horizontal position, can't be lowered close enough to the table for horizontal sawing to be practical, it's necessary to provide a higher support surface for the work. This is done by providing special tables that are secured with the table clamps normally used to lock the fence. Table 1 sits at the right end of the machine and is used to position work while the cutting tool is moved along the arm. With the second concept (table 2 shown in project 13), the motor is in a fixed position against the tool's column so the cutting tool is behind the auxiliary table's fence. Cuts

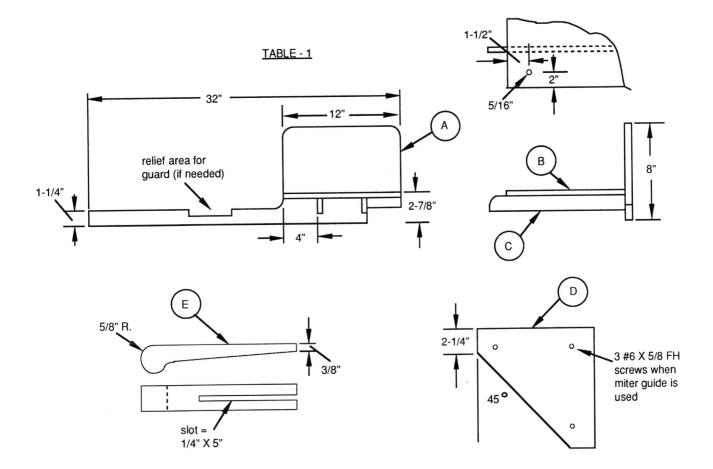

TABLE - 1

relief area for guard (if needed)

3 #6 X 5/8 FH screws when miter guide is used

slot = 1/4" X 5"

that are required at the end of stock, like tenons and spline grooves in miters, are made with table 1. Cuts that are formed along edges of stock, like rabbets and grooves, are accomplished with table 2.

MAKING THE TABLE

STEP 1: MAKE THE FENCE

The fence (A) is a one-piece affair with a "leg" that sits between table boards in place of the tool's fence. Cut the part to shape on a band saw and then smooth all sawed edges. The cutout at the lower right corner of the fence is needed only if the saw is installed between permanent benches. Put the fence in place and judge the location of the relief area in the leg by marking the position of the saw guard.

MATERIALS LIST				
HORIZONTAL TABLE 1				
QTY.	KEY	NAME	SIZE (IN INCHES)	MATERIAL
1	A	Fence	¾ × 8 × 32	Pine
1	B	Table	½ × 12 × 12	Plywood
2	C	Support	¾ × 1½ × 13	Pine
1	D	Miter Guide	¼ × 12 × 12	Hardboard
1	E	Hold-Down	1¼ × 1¼ × 8	Hardwood

No. 6 × ⅝" Flathead Screw (3)   1¼" Sheet Metal Screw (1)

⁵⁄₁₆" × 2" Carriage Bolt with Washer and Wing Nut (1)

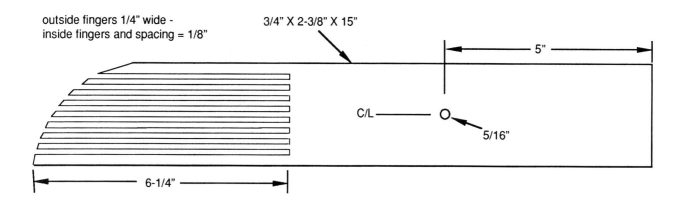

outside fingers 1/4" wide -
inside fingers and spacing = 1/8"

3/4" X 2-3/8" X 15"

5"

C/L — O

5/16"

6-1/4"

STEP 2: ADD THE TABLE AND SUPPORTS

Cut the table (B) and the supports (C) to size and assemble them with glue and 4d finishing nails driven down through the top of the table. Mark the location of the table/support-assembly while the fence is locked in place. Attach the subassembly to the fence with glue and 6d box nails driven through the back of the fence. You can do this while the components are in place on the saw's table. Drill the $5/16''$ hole that is located at the front right corner of the table (see detail on page 83).

STEP 3: ADD THE MITER GUIDE

Prepare the part (D) and make the 45° cut at its left side. Be sure this edge is 45° to the left edge of the table when the guide is attached with the three no. $6 \times 5/8''$ flathead screws.

STEP 4: ADD THE HOLD-DOWN

Make the hold-down from a piece of hardwood 8″ long and 1¼″ square. Form the slot by drilling a ¼″ end-hole and cleaning out the waste on a scroll saw or band saw. Taper the

piece to about 1″ of one end and then round off that end on a disc sander.

STEP 5: MAKE THE SPRING STICK

The spring stick (often called "featherboard"), which is used to hold work against the jig's fence, is secured to the table with the 2″ carriage bolt. Cut the part to size. Drill the $5/16''$ hole and form the kerfs on the table saw before rounding off the end of the part.

USING THE TABLE
SPLINE GROOVES

The workpiece is positioned by the miter guide and secured by the hold-down. The depth of the cut is controlled by the position of the jig in relation to the saw blade. The groove can be kerf-wide for thin splines, or it can be widened by making repeat passes with the blade raised for each one. If you mark one surface on each of the parts involved, and place the parts so that surface faces either up or down on the table, the parts will mesh nicely even if the groove is not exactly centered.

FEATHER GROOVES

The arrangement for sawing feather grooves is the same as the one used for spline grooves, except that the work is positioned as shown in the drawing. You can work with a dadoing tool for wide grooves instead of making repeat passes with a saw blade.

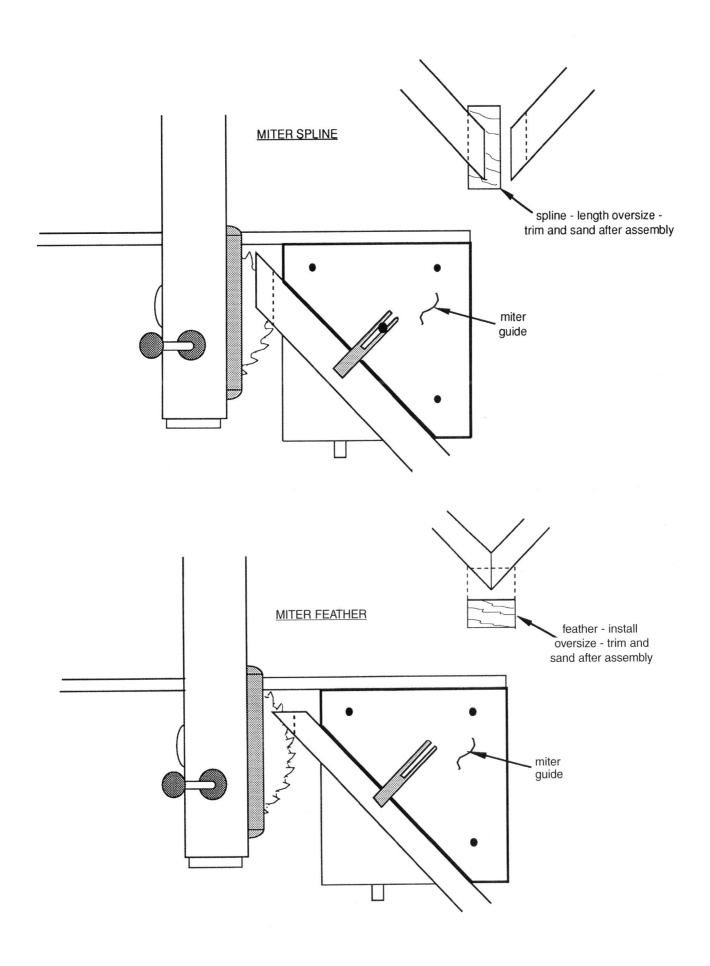

MITER SPLINE

spline - length oversize -
trim and sand after assembly

miter
guide

MITER FEATHER

feather - install
oversize - trim and
sand after assembly

miter
guide

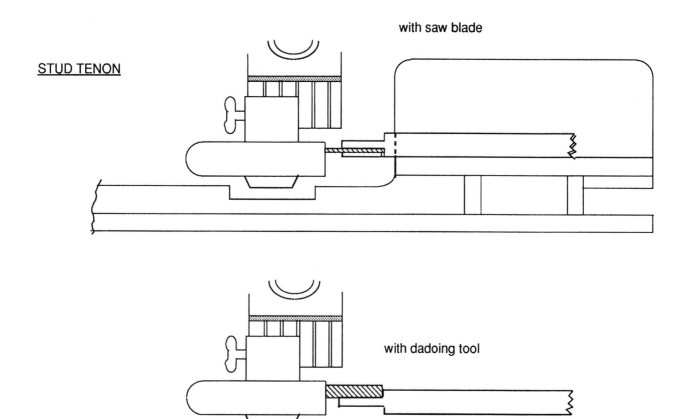

STUD TENON

with saw blade

with dadoing tool

TENONS

Tenons can be formed in one of two ways. Make shoulder cuts first with the tool in normal crosscut position, and then switch to horizontal sawing for the cheek cuts, or, work with a dadoing tool to form the shape in a single pass. When you use the first method, position the work when making the horizontal cuts so the waste falls to the table.

Two-pass method of forming a tenon. The shoulder cuts were made with the machine in normal crosscut mode. Position the work for the cheek cuts so the waste falls to the table. You don't want the cutoff to fall on the spinning blade.

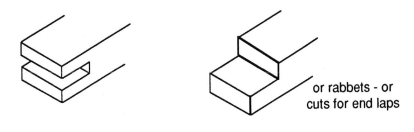

END GROOVE
(with dado)

or rabbets - or
cuts for end laps

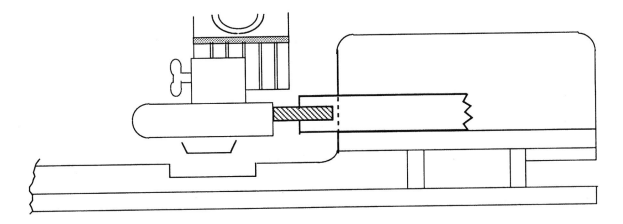

End Grooves or Rabbets

It's best to use a dadoing tool instead of making repeat passes with a saw blade when forming end-grooves or end-rabbets unless you're working with thin stock. Control the depth of the cut on similar pieces by marking the end of the work for alignment with the left edge of the fence. Making test cuts in scrap stock, if centering the groove or establishing the depth-of-cuts for end laps, is critical.

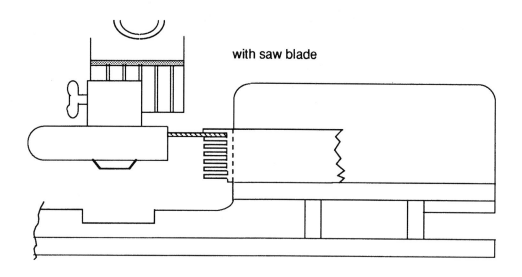

with saw blade

use dadoing tool
for heavier fingers

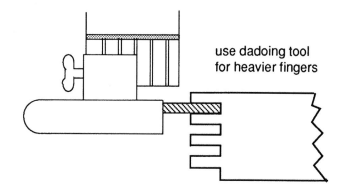

FINGERLAP

The fingerlap joint can be formed
with kerf-wide fingers or heavier ones
if you work with a dadoing tool. Most
carbide-tipped saw blades will form a
⅛″ kerf, but test first to be sure this
is correct. In any case, make test cuts
to determine how many times you
must rotate the arm elevation handle
on the tool to set the correct spacing
between cuts. I need to rotate the
handle on my machine a bit more
than two times in order for fingers
and slots to mesh correctly when I'm
using kerf-wide slots, but that doesn't
guarantee it will work on your machine. Testing is a prerequisite for
satisfactory results.

Adjacent sides of the project are
held together so mating cuts can be

ALIGNING PARTS
FOR FINGERLAP

part 2

part 1

height strip

... part 1 rests on jig's table
... part 2 rests on height strip
... thickness of height strip
    equals width of grooves

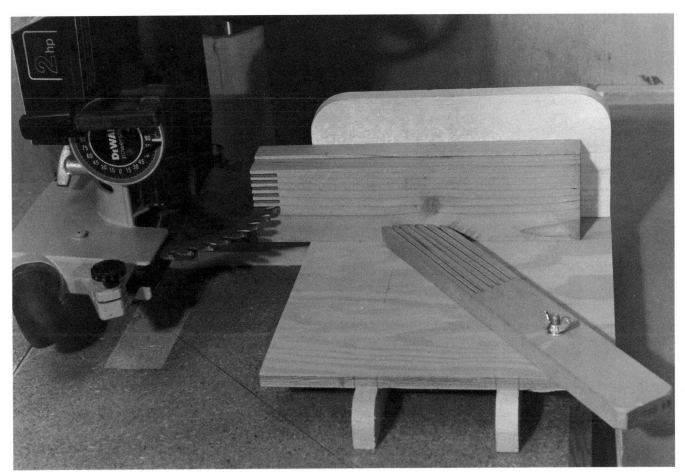

Forming the finger lap with kerf-wide fingers and slots. One of the parts is elevated a slot-width above the mating piece. Note the use of the spring stick. Press it firmly against the work as you tighten the wing nut.

made in one pass, but the parts must be positioned a certain way (see the drawing at the bottom of page 88). One part rests on the jig's table; the second part is elevated on a strip of wood with the thickness equal to the width of a slot.

Successive cuts are made after elevating or lowering the saw blade a distance that is *twice* the width of a slot. Be aware that top and bottom edges of the project will be even only if you establish the width of the parts in increments of the finger-width. For ⅛" fingers, for example, the width of the sides must be 2" or 2⅛", or 4" or 4⅛", and so on.

Radial Arm Saw Horizontal Sawing Table 2

Forming edge rabbets with a dadoing tool. The fingers of the spring stick bear against the work at the right side of the cutting tool. Adjust the guard so it is close to the top surface of the work.

The saw blade is in a fixed position when it is set for use with table 2. Raise the arm of the machine until the blade is well above the table. Rotate the motor to situate the blade in the saw's "in-rip" position; then tilt the motor so the blade will be parallel to the table with its teeth pointing forward. Move the motor toward the column as far as it will go, and secure the position with the rip lock.

Always use the miter gauge to move the work when making cuts at the end of narrow components. A miter gauge with its own hold-down is ideal.

MATERIALS LIST				
HORIZONTAL TABLE 2				
QTY.	KEY	NAME	SIZE (IN INCHES)	MATERIAL
1	A	Table	¾ × 10 × 30	Plywood
2	B	Support	¾ × 1½ × 12	Pine
1	C	Fence	¾ × 6 × 30	Pine
1	D	Spacer	¾ × 2¼ × 30	Pine
2	E	Clamp Ledge	¾ × 1½ × 10½	Pine

⁵⁄₁₆″ × 2″ Carriage Bolt with Washer and Wing Nut (1)

Guard				
QTY.	KEY	NAME	SIZE (IN INCHES)	MATERIAL
1	F	Shield	¾ × 1½ × 8	Pine
1	G	Support	¾ × 3 × 8	Pine

1½″ Sheet Metal Screw with Washer (2)

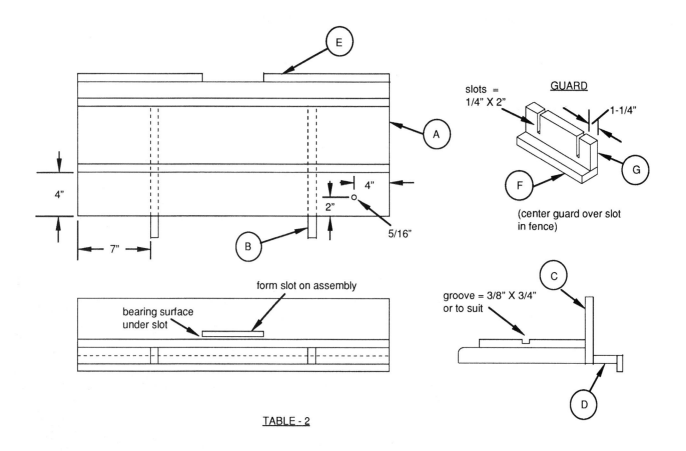

slots =
1/4" X 2"

GUARD

1-1/4"

(center guard over slot in fence)

groove = 3/8" X 3/4"
or to suit

form slot on assembly

bearing surface under slot

TABLE - 2

MAKING THE TABLE

STEP 1: PREPARE CLAMP LEDGES AND SPACER

Cut parts (D) and (E) to size and assemble them with glue and 6d box nails. The space between the clamp ledges provides a relief area for the saw guard. The spacer allows room for the blade when it is in neutral position behind the jig's fence.

STEP 2: MAKE THE FENCE

Cut the fence (C) to size and secure it to the front edge of the spacer with glue and 6d finishing nails. The slot in the fence is made when the jig is complete and in use. It may start as just a kerf with the blade poking through a half-inch or so, but it will be made wider and longer by the cutting tool in use (saw blade or dado) and the operation being performed.

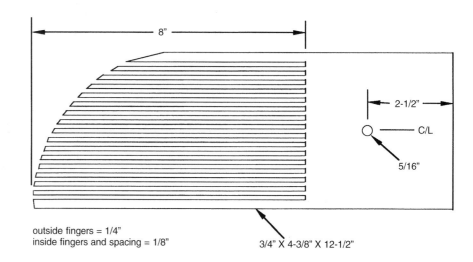

8"

2-1/2"

C/L

5/16"

outside fingers = 1/4"
inside fingers and spacing = 1/8"

3/4" X 4-3/8" X 12-1/2"

STEP 3: TABLE AND SUPPORTS

Saw the table (A) to size and make repeat passes with a saw blade or use a dadoing tool to form the groove for an on-hand miter gauge. The 5/16" hole is for the carriage bolt that will secure a special spring stick.

Make the supports (B) and attach

them to the table with glue and 6d finishing nails that you drive down through the top of the table.

Secure the first assembly (fence, spacer and ledges) in the machine's table with the table clamps and then place the table/support-assembly and mark its location on the fence. Join the two assemblies with glue and 6d box nails driven into the table's edge through the back of the fence. Be sure the table's supports rest firmly on the tool's table.

STEP 4: MAKE THE GUARD

Cut the two parts needed for the guard, and form the slots in the support (G) by drilling end-holes, removing the waste by sawing on a scroll saw or band saw.

Assemble the parts with glue and 6d box nails.

STEP 5: PROVIDE THE SPRING STICK

It's a good idea to cut the part needed for the spring stick longer than necessary so there will be ample room for your hands when you saw the kerfs. Round off the end of the component after the fingers are formed. Then, drill the 5/16″ hole and saw the part to true size.

USING THE TABLE

Hold workpieces flat on the table and snug against the fence when you move them past the cutter (above right). Adjust the cutter, saw blade or dado so it projects the correct distance through the fence, and its height above the table suits the application. Tighten the tool's rip lock after making the adjustments. Keep the saw guard in place (behind the fence) and turn the dust spout so waste will be directed toward the back of the machine.

Position the jig's guard so its shield is close to the top surface of the work; use the spring stick to help keep the work in position as you make the pass.

Always use the miter gauge to move the work when making cuts on the end of narrow components.

TONGUE & GROOVE

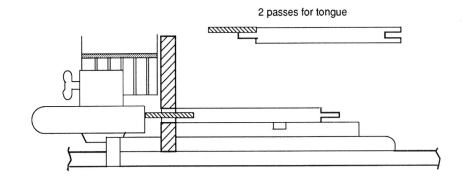

2 passes for tongue

There is enough room between the jig's table and the arm of the saw to allow wide pieces of stock to be positioned on edge. The spring stick isn't shown here, but it should be used to help keep the work against the fence.

Radial Arm Saw Mitering Jig

Frame components, precut to length, are placed in the jig snug against the guide. The cut is made in normal fashion. Pull the blade through the work and then return it to neutral position behind the fence. Allow the blade to stop before removing the work or placing it for a second cut. Always use the lower part of the blade guard even though it isn't shown in the photos.

Forming a 45° miter is a simple chore, but one of the more persnickety sawing jobs because of the absolute accuracy that's required. You might get away with a slight discrepancy in some woodworking areas, but not so with mitering. A slight cut-error, as little as part of a degree, is multiplied by eight when making a square or rectangular frame. So, a little goof evolves as a big error.

Granted, careful setups and test cuts on scrap stock before committing project material can lead to a successful joint, but a jig that consistently positions work correctly and allows the cut to be made like a straightforward crosscut will ensure good results with minimal fuss. The jig I use is easy to install on the machine and, because of a couple of add-ons, is available for compound angle cuts as well as simple as miters.

MAKING THE JIG

STEP 1: TABLE AND FENCE

Prepare the fence and install it on the machine in place of the regular guide. Secure the fence with the table clamps and saw a kerf through it.

Cut the table to size and mark a centerline across its width. Spot the locations for the threaded inserts and drill the four holes. The angle between the table's centerline and the centerline of each pair of holes must be 45°. Install the inserts so they are a bit below the table's surface.

Place the table so its centerline aligns with the kerf in the fence and mark its location on the fence. Join the two components with glue and 6d box nails driven through the rear of the fence, and then place the assembly on the machine so the kerf in the fence lines up with the saw blade. Now, pull the blade forward to extend the kerf across the jig's table.

STEP 2: ADD THE GUIDES

Cut the guides (C) to size and trim their ends to 45°. It isn't critical if the trim cuts are not perfect. Use a draftsman's template to mark 45° angles to the left and right of the kerf. These layout lines *are* critical. Coat the underside of the guides with glue and position them carefully on the table, secure the guides with 4d finishing nails, and check with the 45° template to be sure the guides are placed correctly before driving the nails.

STEP 3: MAKE THE SUPPORTS

Cut the parts for the base and fence to size, and then form the 5⁄16″-wide slots in the base by drilling end-holes and sawing away the waste on a scroll saw or band saw. Join the parts with glue and 6d finishing nails.

Compound cuts are done by placing the support so it braces the work at a specific or arbitrary slope angle. The blade is pulled through as if for a simple crosscut, but the result is a compound angle. This occurs regardless of the work's slope angle.

Some materials, like cove molding, establish their own slope angle. Either of the guides may be used. This is important when the shape of the stock makes it necessary to change its position for the opposing cut.

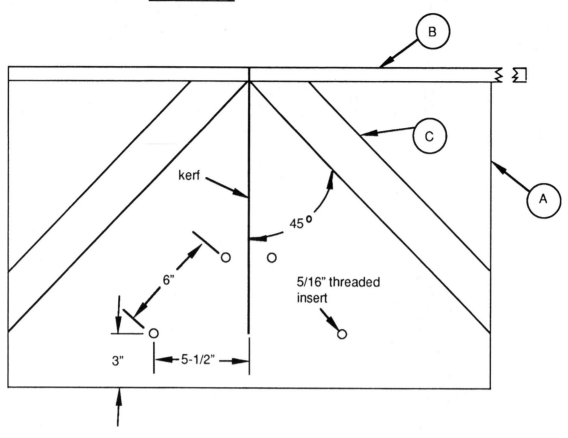

kerf

45°

6"

5/16" threaded insert

3"

5-1/2"

MATERIALS LIST				
MITERING JIG				
QTY.	KEY	NAME	SIZE (IN INCHES)	MATERIAL
1	A	Table	¾ × 17 × 28	Plywood
1	B	Fence	¾ × 2¼ × 36	Pine
2	C	Guides	¾ × 2 × 19½	Pine

⁵⁄₁₆" Threaded Insert (4)

Support				
QTY.	KEY	NAME	SIZE (IN INCHES)	MATERIAL
2	A	Base	¾ × 4 × 9	Pine
2	B	Fence	¾ × 2¼ × 9	Pine

⁵⁄₁₆" × 1½" Bolt with Washer (4)

USING THE JIG

The jig is designed for mitering components that have been precut to length. The system does waste some wood, but eliminates the errors that can occur when parts are cut consecutively from a single piece of material.

Since the jig has left- and right-hand guides, it doesn't matter whether the work is flat or shaped like molding. Moldings, after being sawed at one end, are turned end-for-end and placed against the opposite guide for the second cut.

The jig's support units are used to hold work in position for compound angle cuts. The slope angle of the work can be established with a T-bevel, but many times it can be arbitrary. For example: It isn't a crisis if the slope angle on a shadow box picture frame is plus or minus a few degrees so long as it is visually acceptable. At other times, the material itself, like cove molding, will establish the slope angle.

The jig is fine for much compound angle sawing but it is not a cure-all. Limitations are imposed by the width of the workpiece and the maximum depth-of-cut of the saw blade.

AN EXTRA APPLICATION

The jig is usable for halving or quartering circular or square pieces of stock; however, don't use this technique for very small pieces unless you use double-faced tape, *not your hand*, to keep the work in position.

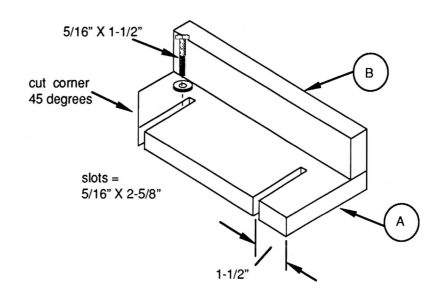

MITER JIG SUPPORTS
make 1 left & 1 right

5/16" X 1-1/2"

cut corner
45 degrees

slots =
5/16" X 2-5/8"

1-1/2"

B

A

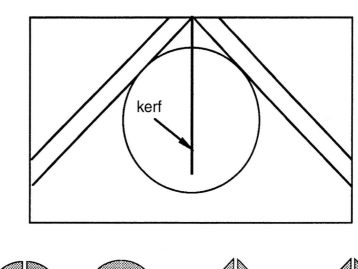

kerf

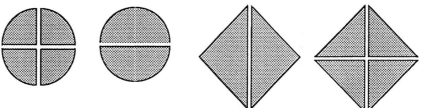

half or quarter discs or squares

Lathe Carriage

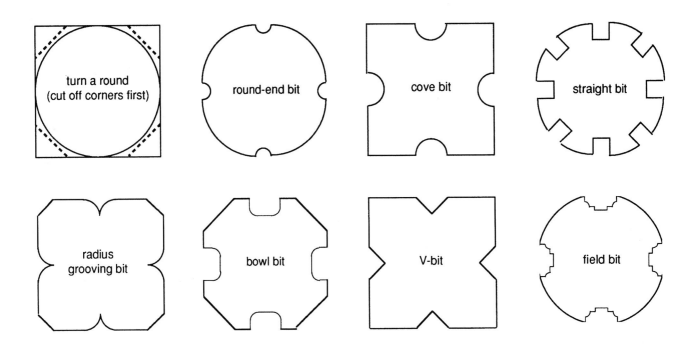

The shapes achieved when doing longitudinal routing with the lathe carriage depends on the bit that is used.

T he parallel ways on most lathe beds seem designed for a jig that enables a portable router—preferably a plunge type—to form longitudinal details on mounted spindles. In addition to doing jobs like fluting and veining, I often use the idea to bring stock to full round (see drawing above).

The lathe's indexing feature is used to position and secure work for flute-type cuts. The router, centered over the work by the jig, is moved from right-to-left. Flats that are needed on a spindle when a leg is attached to a round post, for example, are formed by using a rabbeting bit in the router.

Both the work and the router are in action when turning stock to round.

MAKING THE JIG

The sizes I suggest for parts of the jig, especially the base, are fine for my Delta lathe, but might require some modifying to suit your machine. So check before preparing components for the jig.

STEP 1: PREPARE BASE

Cut the material for the base (A) to size and form ½"-deep × 2⅝"-wide rabbets along each edge. The projection that's left by the rabbet cuts forms a guide that should fit nicely in the space between the lathe's ways. An alternate way to supply the base is to make it in two pieces, the top part ¾" thick, the guide ½" thick. Attach the guide down the center of the top piece with glue and 3d box nails.

STEP 2: ADD THE TIES (DETAIL "B")

Cut the ties (D) to size and install a ¼" threaded insert at the center of each. Drill a ¼" hole O.C., about 2" or so from each end of the base. A thumb screw can be used instead of the round head screw that's shown in the drawing. The ties are used to secure the jig in the lathe.

STEP 3: SUPPLY THE SIDES

Saw the sides (B) to size and form the ⅜"-deep × ¾"-wide rabbet at the bottom edge of each of them. Set up a dadoing tool to cut a bit wider than ¼", and cut the ⅜"-deep grooves at the top of the sides.

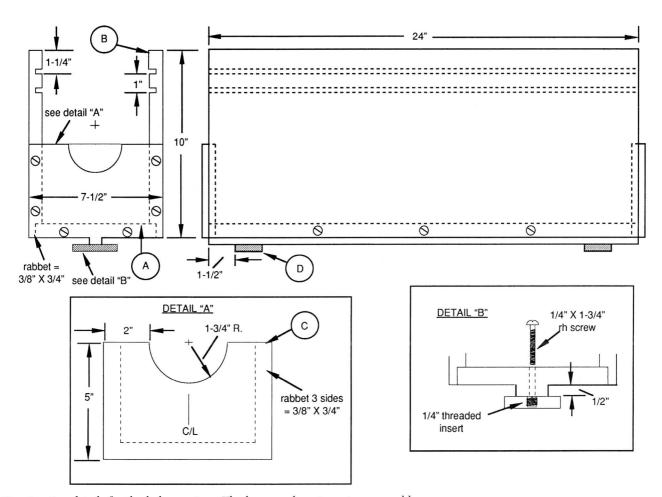

Construction details for the lathe carriage. The base can be a two-piece assembly instead of being formed from a single piece. (See text.)

MATERIALS LIST				
LATHE ROUTER CARRIAGE				
QTY.	KEY	NAME	SIZE (IN INCHES)	MATERIAL
1	A	Base	1½ × 6¾ × 24	Clear Fir
2	B	Sides	¾ × 10 × 24	Clear Fir
2	C	Ends	¾ × 5 × 7½	Clear Fir
2	D	Tie	½ × 1 × 2½	Clear Fir
No. 6 × 1″ Flathead Screws (18)			¼″ × 1¾″ Round Head Screw (2)	
¼″ Threaded Insert (2)				

Join the sides to the base with glue and no. 6 × 1″ flathead screws. Drill adequate pilot and shank holes, and countersink carefully before driving the screws. A good way to prepare the holes quickly and accurately is to use a special bit that's made for screws, like Stanley's "Screw-Mates."

STEP 4: MAKE THE END PIECES (DETAIL "A")

A convenient way to make the ends (C) is to start with a piece that is twice as long as you need and then, using a hole saw or fly cutter, form a 3½″ centered hole. Cut ⅜″-deep × ¾″-wide rabbets on all four edges of the piece before halving it by sawing across the hole's diameter.

Put the ends in place with glue and no. 6 × 1″ flathead screws.

STEP 5: PREPARE THE ROUTER

The best choice of router to use with the carriage is a plunge-type in the medium-power range. Models in the 2½ and up HP range are on the heavy side and might be awkward to handle.

Use tempered hardboard to make the special plate, sizing its width and rounding off its edges so it will move smoothly in the grooves that are in the sides of the carriage. Bore a 1½″ hole at the center of the plate for bits

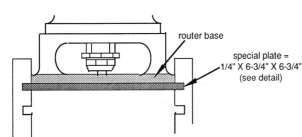

router base

special plate =
1/4" X 6-3/4" X 6-3/4"
(see detail)

form groove wider
by about 1/32"

round off edges
of plate

The grooves in the sides of the
project are a bit wider than the
thickness of the special plate.

to pass through.

Remove the subbase from the
router and, using the same screws
that secured the subbase, attach the
router to the special plate so its chuck
is concentric with the hole.

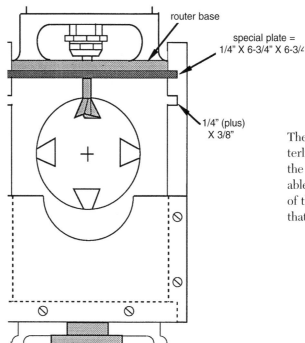

router base

special plate =
1/4" X 6-3/4" X 6-3/4"

1/4" (plus)
X 3/8"

The router moves on the centerline of the workpiece. Use
the grooves that are most suitable in relation to the diameter
of the work and the cut-depth
that's required.

USING THE CARRIAGE

The carriage has an open top so it can
be in place on the lathe before the
workpiece is secured between the
lathe's centers. Secure the carriage
with the ties after its position in relation to the work has been established.

Slide the special plate into the
groove in the sides of the carriage that
best suits the diameter of the work
and the cut-depth that's needed.

Use the lathe's indexing feature to
hold the work in correct position
when making longitudinal cuts. Indexing is also done to rotate the work
$x°$ for ensuing cuts.

Make cuts of limited length by
marking a line across the sides of the
carriage to indicate where to stop.

Shape a workpiece to full round by
setting a lathe speed you would normally use when cutting with lathe
chisels. Chuck an appropriate bit in
the router—a bowl bit, a round nose
bit, even a straight bit will work.
Whatever the bit, start with a light
trim cut and then make successive
passes, cutting a bit deeper each
time.

Judge how deep to cut on any pass
by the way the router behaves; the
tool will protest when you ask too
much of it.

Keep the special plate riding
smoothly in the grooves by occasionally coating its edges and grooves with
paste wax.

Lathe Sled

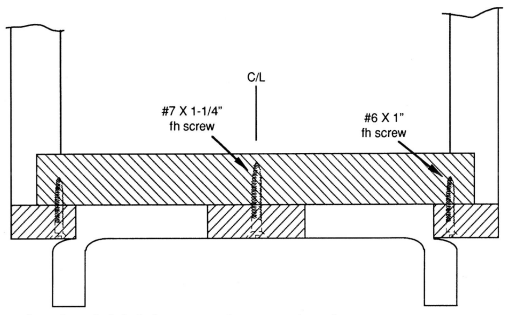

The jig's base must fit nicely on the lathe bed—snug enough to prevent the jig from wobbling while allowing the jig to move smoothly.

The lathe "sled," like the lathe carriage (see page 98), is designed so it can perform with a portable router to make longitudinal cuts on lathe-mounted spindles, but there is a difference. The sled and the router move together; the carriage is locked to the lathe bed while the router is moved. Since the sled slides on the lathe's bed, it can travel almost the full length of the bed, thus affording more flexibility in terms of cut-length.

Because of the project's size, I recommend that it be used with a "small" router. Heavy-duty units of considerable horsepower might be top-heavy and unstable; however, this is not a handicap, since any router will be suitable for the kind of cuts the jig is designed for.

It's important that the base of the jig fit precisely on the lathe bed, so check the dimensions of my unit against your machine and note necessary changes before cutting components.

MAKING THE JIG

STEP 1: START WITH THE BASE ASSEMBLY

Cut the base and the center guide to size. Prepare the guide a bit wider than necessary and then sand one edge until the part fits perfectly in the space between the ways.

Hold the base and guide together with a small clamp at each end and drill suitable holes for three no. 7 × 1¼" flathead screws. Install the screws before removing the clamps. Put the assembly in place on the lathe and test to be sure it moves as it should. An extra step to take— remove and reinstall the screws after coating the contact areas of the guide and base with glue.

Cut the side guides to size and mark where they are attached to the base while the base/guide-assembly is in place on the lathe. Then, clamp the side guides in their correct location and drill suitable holes for the no. 6 × 1" flathead screws. Install the screws before removing the clamps. Put the assembly in place on the lathe and test to be sure it slides smoothly on the ways. Then you can take the "extra" step—remove and reinstall the screws after coating contact areas of base and guides with glue.

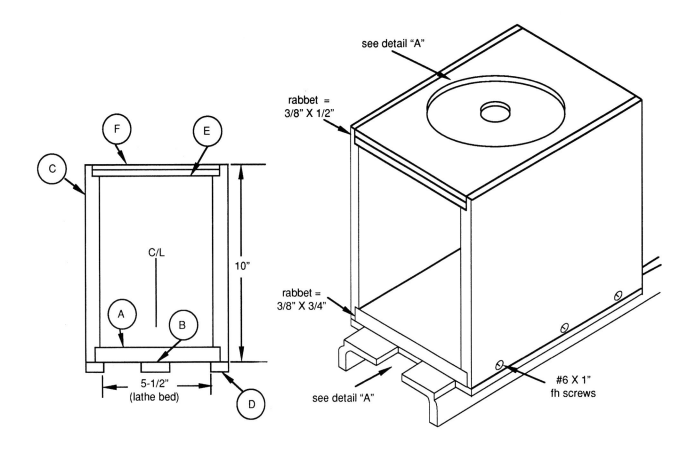

Construction details for the complete jig. The 10″ height is appropriate for my lathe. The sides can be shorter if that would be more suitable for your machine.

MATERIALS LIST				
LATHE "SLED"				
QTY.	KEY	NAME	SIZE (IN INCHES)	MATERIAL
1	A	Base	¾ × 6¾ × 10	Hardwood
1	B	Center Guide	½ × 1½ × 10	Hardwood
2	C	Sides	¾ × 8½ × 10	Plywood
2	D	Side Guide	½ × 1 × 10	Hardwood
1	E	Bottom Plate	¼ × 6¾ × 10	Hardboard
1	F	Top Plate	¼ × 6¾ × 10	Hardboard
No. 7 × 1¼″ Flathead Screw (3)			No. 6 × 1″ Flathead Screw (12)	

STEP 2: ADD THE SIDES

Prepare the parts for the sides and then form a ⅜″-deep × ¾″-wide rabbet on one edge and a ⅜″-deep × ½″-wide rabbet on the opposite edge.

Join each side to the base with glue and three no. 6 × 1″ flathead screws. Be sure the angle between the base and the sides is 90°.

STEP 3: SUPPLY THE TOP

Saw one of the plates to size and bore the 1½″ centered hole. Decide how you will form the large hole in the top plate before cutting it to size. If you plan to form the hole on a scroll saw, the consideration doesn't matter. But if you wish to work with a fly cutter in the drill press, cut the part substantially oversize so it can be clamped together with a backing board to the drill press table. Run the fly cutter at lowest speed and keep hands well away from the cutting tool. Saw the part to size after the hole is formed.

If scroll-sawing, form the hole slightly undersize and then use a drum sander to bring it to true diameter. In any case, size the hole so it will provide a tight fit for the router's subbase.

Coat the contact areas of the two plates with glue and keep them together with clamps until the glue sets.

Coat the edges of the plate-assembly and the top edges of the jig's sides with glue and put the plates in place. Place a weight on top of the plates and use small bar clamps to apply light pressure from the sides of the jig.

USING THE JIG

Clean the surface of the lathe-ways and polish them with paste wax. Also apply wax to the bottom of the jig.

Put the jig in place before mounting the work between centers. Use the lathe's indexer to secure the position of the work and to rotate it to whatever degree is needed for subsequent cuts.

Apply downward pressure on the jig as you move it slowly forward for the cut. Making deep cuts in a single pass is not good practice; make repeat passes, lowering the cutter a bit for each one.

To control the length of cuts, clamp a strip of wood across the lathe bed to serve as a stop.

Make cuts on the circumference of the work by using a small clamp to secure the jig, at its base, to one of the ways. Adjust the lathe speed to whatever is appropriate for the size of the work and lower the bit to make contact. Both the lathe and the jig are in action.

DETAIL "B"

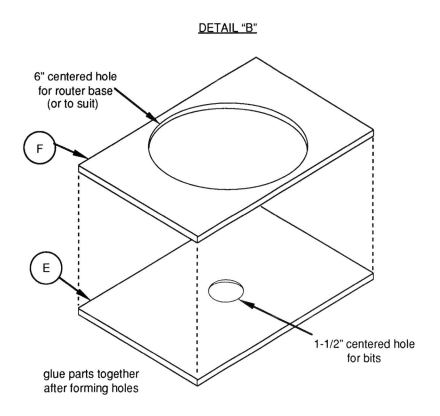

6" centered hole for router base (or to suit)

F

E

1-1/2" centered hole for bits

glue parts together after forming holes

The hole in the top plate should provide a fairly tight fit for the router's subbase. Contact cement can be used instead of glue to join the two parts.

Disc Sander Pivot Jig

Mount the pivot jig for the disc sander so work is held against the "down" side of the disc. Move the jig occasionally to utilize the entire abrasive surface of the disc. Hold the jig in place with a small clamp.

The disc sander is not exempt from machines whose functions can be exploited or extended by a jig—in this case a pivot jig. But I use my jig for more than sanding edges on circular components. Bringing an oval shape to final form, rounding off the end or the corners of a part, sanding a curved segment to uniform width, are all part of the program. A plus factor of the jig is that when doing any of the chores, you can ensure duplication when you need similar components.

MAKING THE JIG

STEP 1: PREPARE THE BASE AND TOP PARTS

Saw the base (A) and parts (B) and (C) to the sizes shown in the materials list. Do not form the end tapers at this time. Bevel-saw one edge of the top pieces to 45°. Attach the top left-hand part to the base with glue and 3d finishing nails, driving the nails up through the base. Do not place nails in the area of the taper cut that will be made later.

STEP 2: MAKE THE SLIDE

The slide is made at this point of the construction, because it will be used to position the top right-hand component. Prepare the part needed for the slide and bevel its edges to 45°. This is a narrow piece, so be sure to use a pusher to move it past the saw blade.

Mark the centerline of the slide and install the four ³⁄₁₆″ threaded inserts. Install the inserts from the top so they are flush with the slide's surface.

STEP 3: FINISH THE ASSEMBLY

Place the slide against the top left-hand part (already installed on the base) and position the right-hand piece so it butts lightly against the slide. Secure the part to the base with glue and 3d finishing nails.

Draw the lines for the tapers and work on a scroll saw or band saw to remove the waste. Smooth the sawed edges by sanding.

Install the ¼″ threaded insert on the centerline of the dovetail groove an inch or so from the rear of the jig.

Place the jig on the tool's table so its front edge is parallel to and ⅛″ away from the sanding disc. Mark the location of the guide (D) and attach it to the jig with glue and 3d finishing

Pivot points can be used in any of the threaded inserts in the slide. Use the blunt point when the work has a center hole. Work that does not have a center hole is simply impaled on the pointed pivot.

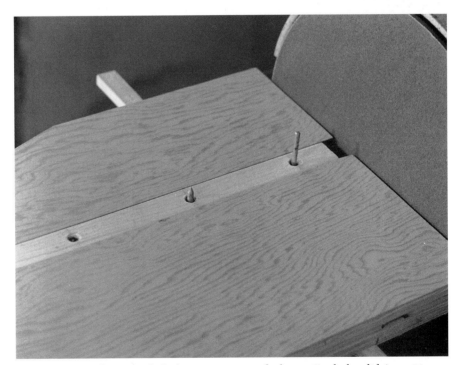

Workpieces can be rotated clockwise or counterclockwise. Lock the slide's position after you have moved the work to contact the disc. Several light passes are better than a single heavy one. The jig allows sanding circles from 1½″ to more than 24″ in diameter.

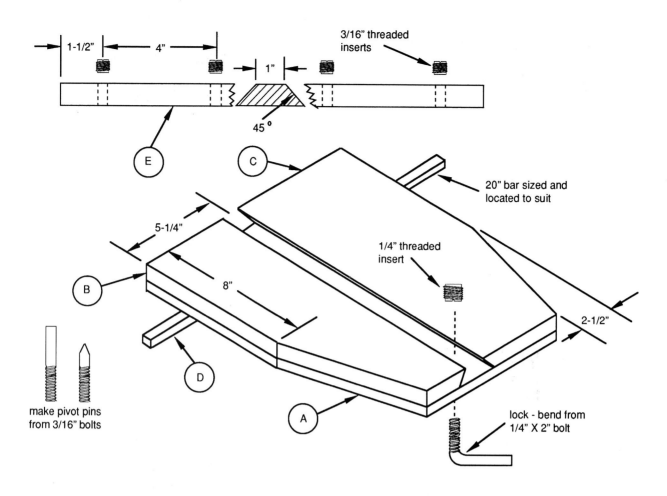

3/16" threaded inserts

1-1/2" 4" 1"

20" bar sized and located to suit

45°

E C

5-1/4"

1/4" threaded insert

B

8"

D

A

2-1/2"

make pivot pins from 3/16" bolts

lock - bend from 1/4" X 2" bolt

MATERIALS LIST				
ROUTER PIVOT JIG				
QTY.	KEY	NAME	SIZE (IN INCHES)	MATERIAL
1	A	Top Plate	½ × 7½ × 12½	Plywood
1	B	Bottom Plate	½ × 7½ × 12½	Plywood
1	C	Long Slide	½ × 1½ × 14	Hardwood
1	D	Short Slide	½ × 1½ × 7	Hardwood
8/32 Threaded Insert (5)			10/32 × ¾" Round Head Screw (1)	
10/32 Threaded Insert (1)			8/32 × ¾" Round Head Screw (2)	

USING THE JIG
SANDING CIRCULAR PIECES

Mount the work on a pivot and move the slide until the work-edge touches the sanding disc. Lock the slide's position and turn on the machine. The work may be rotated either clockwise or counterclockwise. When you need duplicates, say, for a set of wheels, mark the slide's position so it can be repositioned accurately.

ROUNDING ENDS

Mark one or two pivot points depending on whether the part will be shaped at one or both ends. If the curve is slight, butt the work lightly against the disc before securing the slide. For a more pronounced curve, saw off the waste before doing the sanding.

nails. If the table lacks a miter gauge groove, the jig can be held in place with small clamps or even strips of carpet tape.

FINAL STEP: SUPPLY THE HARDWARE

Make the pivot points by using a hacksaw to remove the heads from a pair of ³⁄₁₆″ screws. Use the blunt one when the work has a center hole, the pointed one, that is made by chucking the screw in the drill press and working on it with a file, allows rotating work that does not have a hole. The workpiece is simply impaled on the point.

Make the lock by removing the head from a ¼″ × 2″ bolt and then bending the bolt into an L-shape.

ROUND OFF ENDS OF STOCK

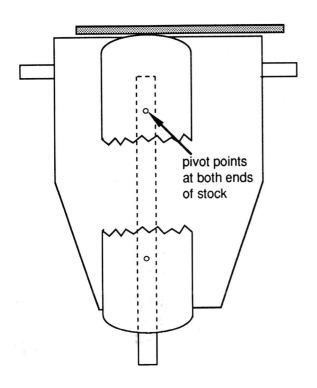

pivot points at both ends of stock

ROUND OFF CORNERS

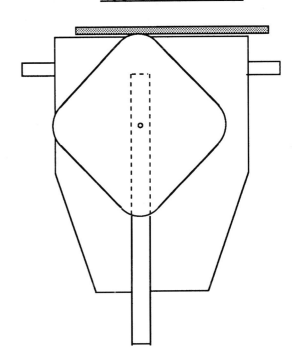

OVAL SHAPES

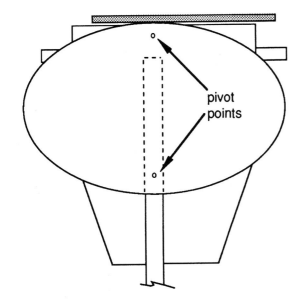

pivot points

ROUNDING CORNERS

A single pivot point is required when rounding off the corners of square pieces. Preshape the corners by sawing if you must remove a lot of material.

OVAL SHAPES

Two pivot points are needed to sand oval shapes. Establish the point locations by marking the horizontal and vertical axes of the part's shape, either on paper or the work itself. If the shape is critical, do a test on scrap stock before committing good material.

SANDING CURVES TO WIDTH

Make a special post for this application by drilling a concentric hole in the end of a ⅜″ × 1½″ steel bar, and tapping the hole for the threaded portion of a ³⁄₁₆″ screw. The post is installed in one of the inserts in the slide.

Lock the slide so the distance from the post to the sanding disc equals the desired width of the work. The first step is to sand the inside edge of the work on a drum sander. Then, move the work between the post and the disc, turning the work constantly to maintain the contact point.

AN EXTRA— CHAMFERING JIG FOR DOWELS

Cut a 10″ length of 2×4 and on the centerline of one edge, use brad-point bits to drill holes for various dowel diameters. Size the holes accurately so the dowels will move easily but without wobble.

Clamp the jig to the sander's table at the angle that's needed, and pass the dowel through the appropriate hole. Move the dowel to contact the abrasive surface and rotate it slowly, counterclockwise. A light touch works best.

You can form bevels or flat-sided points by holding the dowel steady as you move it forward. If the dowels fit too tightly, try coating them lightly with paste wax.

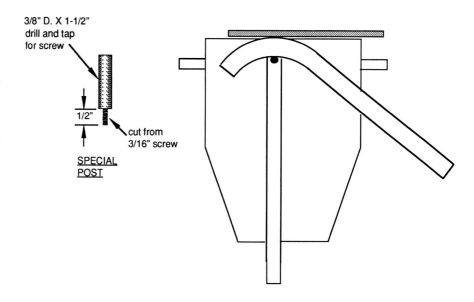

SAND CURVES TO WIDTH

3/8" D. X 1-1/2"
drill and tap
for screw

1/2"

cut from
3/16" screw

SPECIAL
POST

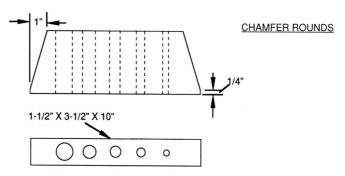

CHAMFER ROUNDS

1"

1/4"

1-1/2" X 3-1/2" X 10"

holes on centerline -- spaced
1-1/2" -- sizes 1", 3/4", 5/8",
1/2", 3/8" (or to suit)

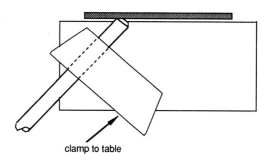

clamp to table

Stationary Belt Sander Jigs

The advantage of the belt sander is its "in-line" action; surface-, edge- or end-sanding can be accomplished without the swirl marks left by many other sanding tools. It's exceptionally useful for use with a homemade guide for the final touch on miter cuts whether the work is held flat or on edge.

Too often, the tool is limited to smoothing relatively small components. This may be due to the fact that its standard table is situated so only a section of the abrasive belt is available. I've learned also that many woodworkers overlook the advantages of using the tool in its horizontal mode. I use the arrangement with a special "stop" substituting for the table, or with a fence that's situated parallel to the belt. The setup allows sanding long stock—longer than would be possible otherwise.

MAKING A MITER JIG

STEP 1: PREPARE THE BASE AND GUIDE

The jig is designed for a 6"-wide belt. Change the sizes of the components to suit if you have a smaller unit.

Saw the base to size, then place it on the tool's table so it is centered, with its forward edge ⅛" away from the belt. Mark the location of the table's slot; size the guide to suit the slot, and attach it to the jig's base with glue and 3d finishing nails.

STEP 2: FENCES AND SUPPORTS

Cut the fences to size and saw a 45° bevel on one end of each. Place the fences on the base and mark their locations with a combination square or draftsman's 45° template.

Saw the supports to size. The drawing shows a point on the free end of the supports, but the shape isn't critical. Leaving the ends square won't interfere with function. Hold the fences in correct position and mark the location of the supports. Assemble the components with glue and 4d finishing nails driven through the face of the fences.

Apply glue to the bottom edges of the support/fence assemblies and clamp them carefully in correct position on the base. Secure the assemblies by driving 4d finishing nails up through the base.

MATERIALS LIST				
NO. 2 CENTERING JIG				
QTY.	KEY	NAME	SIZE (IN INCHES)	MATERIAL
1	A	Base	³⁄₁₆ or ¼ × 7 × 12¼	Acrylic or Hardboard
2	B	Guide	⅜ × 1½ × 7	Hardwood
8/24 × ¾" Machine Screw (4)			Washers (4)	
8/24 Wing Nut (4)				

USING THE MITER JIG

The jig is usable for finishing surface or edge miters. Move the jig occasionally to avoid working on just one section of the abrasive. Since the project has left- and right-hand fences, opposite ends of material that can't be flipped—like molding—can be sanded.

"INCREASING" THE ABRASIVE SURFACE

The abrasive area of the belt, of course, is constant, but with the regular table in place you can use only a section of it. By using an L-shaped stop instead of the table, most of the sanding area becomes available.

The stop, made along the lines shown at the top of page 111, is attached with bolts put through existing holes or, if possible, with clamps. The stop, usable whether the sander is in vertical or horizontal position, is good to use when the work is no longer than the machine's platen. Hold the work firmly against the stop. Little pressure is needed; the work's weight is usually enough to get the job done. Be careful with hand-placement, especially when sanding thin pieces.

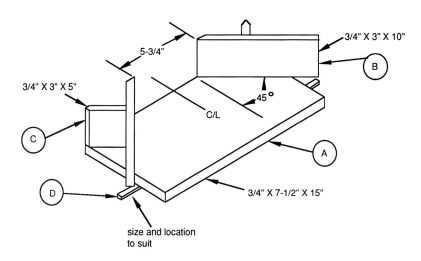

BELT SANDER MITER JIG

3/4" X 3" X 10"

5-3/4"

3/4" X 3" X 5"

45°

C/L

3/4" X 7-1/2" X 15"

size and location to suit

Construction details of a mitering jig for a belt sander.

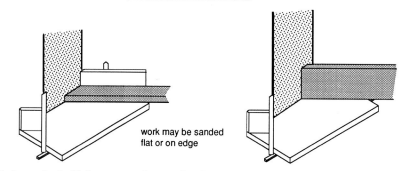

BELT SANDER JIG AT WORK

work may be sanded flat or on edge

Work can be held flat or on edge. Make the saw cuts so little sanding is needed to finish the edges. Move the jig occasionally to avoid overusing a limited area of the abrasive.

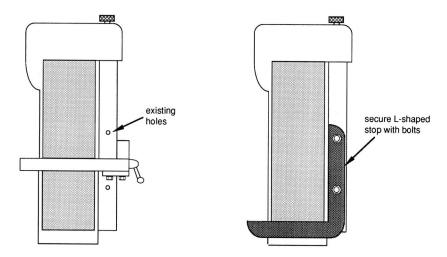

CUSTOM STOP

existing holes

secure L-shaped stop with bolts

The standard table limits the usable abrasive area. The L-shaped stop allows sanding longer pieces of work. The stop may be used with the tool in vertical or horizontal position.

PARALLEL FENCES

Parallel fences, like those below, are custom-made to suit the machine. They can be straight, or shaped at one end to suit the circumference of the tool's idler drum. Actually, if you opt for the latter design, it can be used for straight or drum sanding; drum sanding being made available by removing the cover of the idler drum.

L-STOP

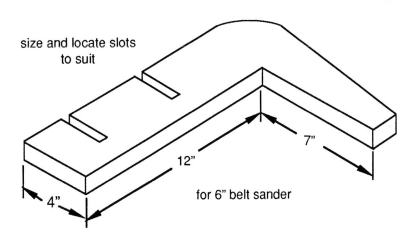

size and locate slots to suit

12"

7"

4"

for 6" belt sander

Size the L-shaped stop to suit the machine. Most belt sanders have holes for attachment of after-market accessories. If not, you may be able to drill and tap a couple of holes or use clamps.

PARALLEL FENCES

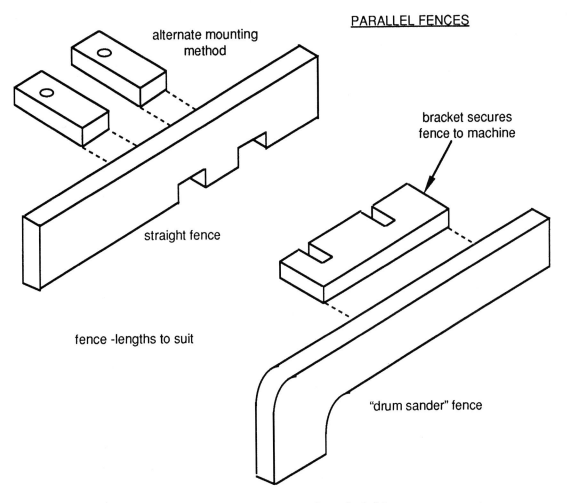

alternate mounting method

straight fence

fence -lengths to suit

bracket secures fence to machine

"drum sander" fence

Designs for custom-made fences. Situate them so they are ⅛" or so above the belt's surface. If necessary, use a heavy washer between the bracket and the machine.

The fences are used to guide work for surface sanding. Use a pusher hold-down to control and move work that is no longer than the tool's platen (see drawing at right). Long components can be surface-sanded, see drawing below, but be aware of the belt's tendency to move the work with it. Good procedure is to use one hand lightly on the surface of the work to maintain contact between work and drum; the other hand at the end of the work to move it forward. Stand at the side of the machine; then, if you lose control of the work, it won't move toward you.

Use the fence to guide work when sanding edges. In this case, there is ample opportunity to control the work by placing hands on the top edge of the work well away from the belt.

USE PUSHER-HOLD-DOWN

Use a pusher hold-down when surfacing stock that is no longer than the tool's platen. Keep light pressure on the work as you move it against the belt's direction of travel.

LONG WORK

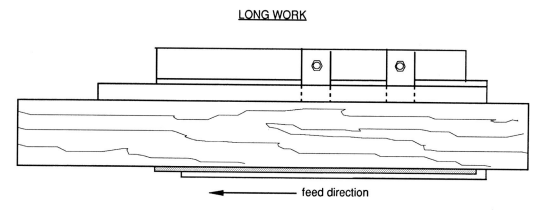

Handle long stock with care. Always be aware that the belt tends to move the work in its own direction of travel.

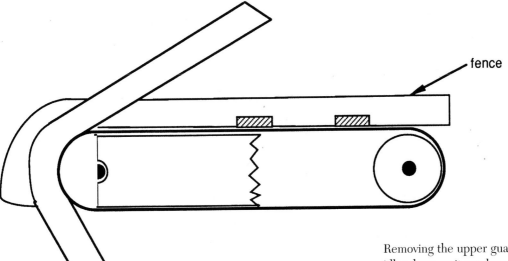

fence

Removing the upper guard exposes the idler drum so it can be used for drum sanding. Move work against the belt's rotation. In this view, the belt is moving clockwise, so work is moved "downward."

Surface-sanding on work that is wider than than the belt can be done by feeding the work diagonally across the belt. Secure the fence with a single fastener. Angle the fence away from the belt the least amount possible that still permits full contact between work and belt. Feed the work against the belt's direction of rotation. This is cross-grain sanding no matter how fine a belt you use, so the job must be finished by sanding with the grain by hand or with a portable pad sander.

Smoothing inside curves on the belt sander is feasible, as long as the radius of the curves is no smaller than that of the idler drum. Use the fence to maintain the work's position so sanded edges will be square to adjacent surfaces (see drawing above). The belt sander is an aggressive machine, so use a light touch and move the work steadily against the belt's direction of travel.

Router Circle Cutting Jig

The project, ready for the router. The jig is designed so the slide can be brought close to the router bit. This accounts for why it can be used for small diameter holes or discs.

The jig is always ready to go without the nuisance of having to secure the router with screws. Size the hole in the top plate to provide a snug fit for the tool's subbase.

The first circle-cutting jig (pivot jig) I made for a portable router was as modest as you can get. Just a strip of wood with the router attached at one end and a series of holes on a common centerline so a nail could be used as a pivot point. It was crude and served the purpose for a while, but the pivot holes soon became ragged, and it was annoying to have to mount the router each time I needed to form a hole or prepare a disc. Also, while I could form large holes or discs, the arrangement was limited at the small-diameter end.

My current version is more sophisticated. The pivot holes won't wear, the pivot point can be set close to the router bit for small holes, the distance from the pivot point to the bit is infinitely adjustable, and I just pop the router into place and go.

MAKING THE JIG

STEP 1: TOP AND BOTTOM PLATES

Prepare the plates (A) and (B) to the sizes shown in the materials list. Identify the parts as top plate (A) and bottom plate (B) and draw a centerline down the length of each of them.

Mark a point on the centerline of the top plate 3¾" from one end. Use the point as the center of a circle that will provide a snug fit for the router's subbase. Form the hole by using a fly cutter in a drill press or by sawing it out on a scroll saw. If you use a fly

The workpiece doesn't require special attention when routing a groove. Clamp the work and a backup to the bench when cutting through to form a hole or a disc. Finish deep or heavy cuts by making repeat passes, projecting the bit a little more for each of the cuts.

I use the pivot jig when I want to shape the edge of a circular component. You just have to be careful about setting the radius of the cut. My Black & Decker router has a nice bit-projection system. I turn the knob for depth-of-cut after the router is in place.

The circle-cutting jig will form large or small holes or discs. Maximum radius capacity is better than 24″.

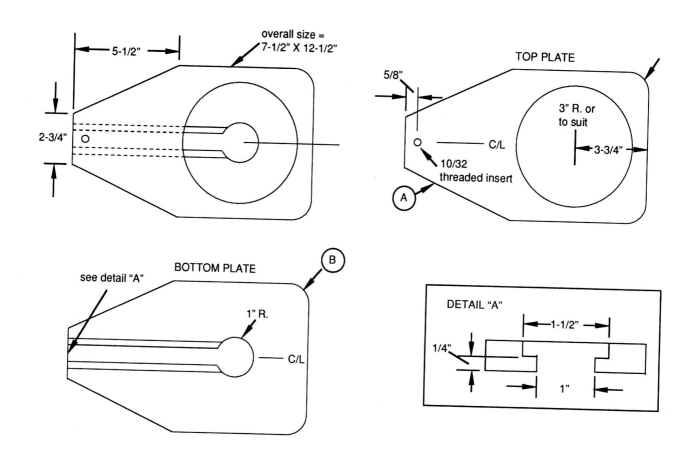

MATERIALS LIST				
ROUTER PIVOT JIG				
QTY.	KEY	NAME	SIZE (IN INCHES)	MATERIAL
1	A	Top Plate	½ × 7½ × 12½	Plywood
1	B	Bottom Plate	½ × 7½ × 12½	Plywood
1	C	Long Slide	½ × 1½ × 14	Hardwood
1	D	Short Slide	½ × 1½ × 7	Hardwood
8/32 Threaded Insert (5)			10/32 × ¾″ Round Head Screw (1)	
10/32 Threaded Insert (1)			8/32 × ¾″ Round Head Screw (2)	

cutter, be sure the work and a backing block are clamped to the machine's table. Run the cutter at lowest speed, and keep hands well away from the cutting area. Saw inside the line if you work with a scroll saw; finish to the line with a drum sander.

Install the 10/32 threaded insert on the plate's centerline ⅝″ in from the edge opposite the hole.

Make a layout on the bottom plate for a 1″ hole that will be concentric with the hole in the top plate. Form the hole with a Forstner or brad-point bit.

STEP 2: T-SHAPED GROOVE IN THE BOTTOM PLATE

Use a dadoing tool or make repeat passes with a saw blade to form a ¼″-deep × 1½″-wide groove down the centerline of the plate. Then, saw

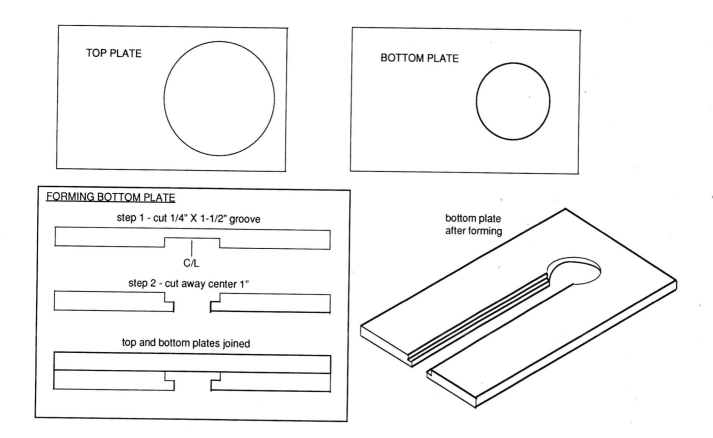

FORMING BOTTOM PLATE

step 1 - cut 1/4" X 1-1/2" groove

C/L

step 2 - cut away center 1"

top and bottom plates joined

bottom plate
after forming

away a 1″-wide section from the center of the groove. The cuts end at the hole that is in the plate.

STEP 3: ASSEMBLE THE PLATES

Coat the contact areas of the two plates with glue and hold them together with clamps. Be sure the wide section of the T-slot in the bottom plate is against the bottom of the top plate. Wait for the glue to set before going further, or speed up production by holding the parts together with ¾″ brads. Place the brads so they won't interfere with final shaping of the assembly.

Mark the lines of the taper cuts and saw away the waste on a scroll saw or band saw. Sand the sawed edges smooth, and round off the rear corners of the assembly on a disc sander.

STEP 4: PREPARE THE SLIDES

I made two slides for my unit, feeling that a short slide might be more convenient on particular applications. It's not critical that you do so. If you make two, start with parent stock that is 22″ or so long. Cut the piece into suitable lengths after the edges are rabbeted.

The rabbets are ¼″-wide × ¼″-deep. Form them by making repeat passes with a saw blade or by using a dadoing tool. Be sure to use a push stick to move the material past the cutting tool. Check the fit of the slides in the plate-assembly. Do some judicious sanding, if necessary, so they will move smoothly and without wobble.

Draw a longitudinal centerline on the slide (or slides) and mark the location of the threaded inserts on the

centerline. Drill the holes for the inserts and install them so they will be flush with the top surface of the slide.

Make the pivot point by removing the head from an 8/32 × ¾″ screw. Chuck the screw in the drill press and shape a point on its end with a file. Alternately, hold the screw in a portable drill and spin it against a turning grinding wheel. Use the grinder's shield, and wear safety goggles!

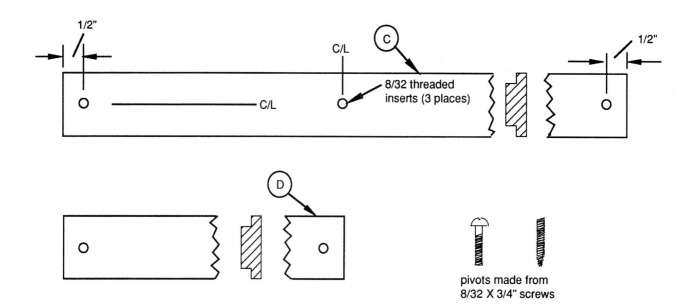

8/32 threaded
inserts (3 places)

pivots made from
8/32 X 3/4" screws

USING THE JIG

The project, like all pivot jigs, works best with a plunge router since the bit can be lowered for the cut after the router is in place.

Set the pivot point at the center of the circular cut that's needed; in a hole if there is one, or simply press it into place. The distance from the pivot point to the bit (the radius of the cut) depends on the operation. Set the distance from the pivot point to the *closest* side of the bit when forming a disc. Set the distance to the *furthest* side of the cutter when routing a hole.

Secure the position of the slide with the round head screw that threads into the insert in the top plate. Don't over-tighten the screw; slight pressure against the slide is enough to keep the slide in place.

Place one hand on the slide at the pivot point, use the other hand to move the router.

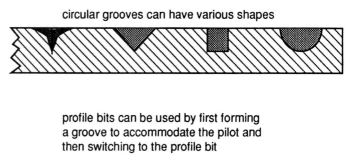

circular grooves can have various shapes

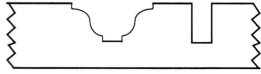

profile bits can be used by first forming a groove to accommodate the pilot and then switching to the profile bit

Piloted profile bits can be used to form decorative circular groove if a straight bit is used first to accommodate the bit's pilot. Field bits do not have pilots, so they can be used without preliminary preparation.

Portable Router Centering Jigs

A centering jig allows forming grooves, dovetails or mortises, down the center of stock-edges, and surfaces too, if the component's width is not beyond the jig's capacity. Other than mounting the jig on the router, there's little fussing involved in producing accurate work. I made two versions of centering jigs because I found that just one type is not suitable for every chore I encountered. One jig is equipped with roller bearings that straddle the workpiece to keep the router bit centered. The second jig has adjustable guides so it can be adjusted for off-center cuts as well as centered ones.

MAKING JIG 1

STEP 1: MAKE A SPECIAL BASE

Use tempered hardboard—or acrylic if you prefer—to make a disc with diameter equal to that of the router's subbase. Mark an accurate diameter on the disc and, at its center, bore a 1″ centered hole through the disc.

Using the router's subbase as a template, carefully locate and drill the mounting holes for the substitute base. You may be able to use original screws to attach the new base; if not, supply new, flathead screws so they can be set flush with the bottom surface of the base.

STEP 2: ADD THE BEARINGS

Mark the location of the screws that hold the bearings on the disc's diameter, ½″ away from the disc's edge. Do this carefully, since it's important that the bearings be equidistant from the router's vertical centerline. Drill the holes and countersink them so the screws will seat flush with the top surface of the disc.

Place a washer between the bearing and the base; secure the bearing with a lock nut.

USING THE JIG

The bearings, straddling the work, will automatically center the bit on the workpiece. Hold and move the router so the contact point between work and bearings is consistent. Clamp strips of wood to the sides of the workpiece, when necessary, to provide adequate support for the router.

The jig can be used for mortising, but the application is limited, since the jig can't be used near the end of stock—both bearings must be in contact with the work. However, there are solutions: "Thicken" the component, so the jig can straddle it, by clamping strips of wood to its sides; or, start with a piece that is longer than necessary, and trim it to length after the mortise is formed.

MATERIALS LIST				
NO. 2 CENTERING JIG				
QTY.	KEY	NAME	SIZE (IN INCHES)	MATERIAL
1	A	Base	$\frac{3}{16}$ or $\frac{1}{4} \times 7 \times 12\frac{1}{4}$	Acrylic or Hardboard
2	B	Guide	$\frac{3}{8} \times 1\frac{1}{2} \times 7$	Hardwood
8/24 × ¾″ Machine Screw (4)			Washers (4)	
8/24 Wing Nut (4)				

MAKING JIG 2

STEP 1: PREPARE THE BASE

Saw a piece of acrylic plastic (or hardboard) to the size shown in the materials list and mark it with horizontal and vertical centerlines. Use a compass at the intersection of the lines to draw a circle with a diameter that equals that of the router base without the subbase. Use the intersection of the lines as a center, and bore a 1" hole through the part.

Drill ³⁄₁₆" end-holes for the slots, and then remove the waste by sawing on a scroll saw or band saw.

Use the router's subbase as a template to locate the holes that will be used to attach the substitute base to the router. Use the original flathead screws to install the new base, or supply longer ones, if necessary. In either case, countersink the holes so the screws can be installed flush with the bottom surface of the base.

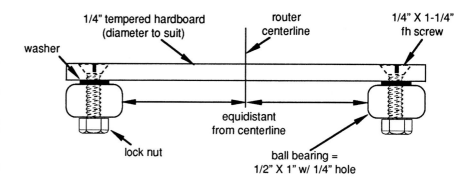

Construction details for the ball bearing centering jig.

AT WORK

rotate router so bearings ride against sides of work

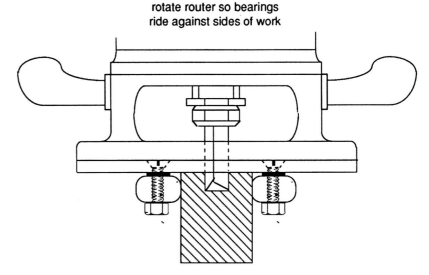

The bearings guide the router smoothly along the work. The jig works best for intermediate cuts on the work.

STEP 2: MAKE THE GUIDES

Prepare the wood for the guides and mark a centerline along their length. Mark the location of the two holes on the centerline of the guides, being sure that the holes will line up with the slots in the base.

USING THE JIG

The jig can be preset by positioning the guides equidistant from the center of the workpiece. For off-center cuts, set one guide to establish the edge distance of the cut before adjusting the second guide.

An advantage of this design is that the guides are parallel and they extend far enough ahead of the cutter to allow situating the jig at or on the end of workpieces. Thus, for one thing, mortising can be done near the end of components.

Both jigs work best with a plunge router, since the design permits positioning the router before the bit is projected to contact the work.

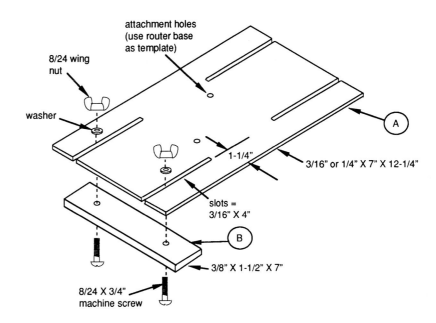

Components of the no. 2 centering jig. The base can be acrylic or hardboard.

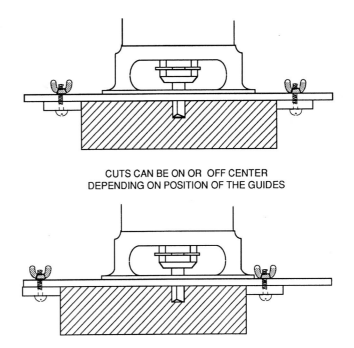

The no. 2 jig has greater capacity than the ball bearing version. It's available for cutting into surfaces as well as edges of material.

Portable Router Spline Groove Jig

The miter is an exemplary woodworking joint because it turns a corner without revealing the end-grain of the components. It leaves a pleasant joint-line but lacks strength. The glue area of a miter isn't much more than that of a butt joint, and an end-grain-to-end-grain connection isn't often recommended; so, reinforcement is in order—the most popular option being a spline. Splines perform correctly and they add a decorative detail if made from a contrasting material.

The grooves for splines can be formed with a dadoing tool or by making repeat passes with a saw blade. The methods are functional, but require some fussing to be sure the grooves are of correct width. The spline groove jig is designed to work with a router. The advantage of router bits is that they are precise. To form a groove of particular width, you just choose a bit of suitable diameter.

The jig's fence is adjustable, so the router can be positioned to form a centered groove regardless of the work's thickness. An outboard support (extension table) keeps the router on an even keel (see the drawing on page 123).

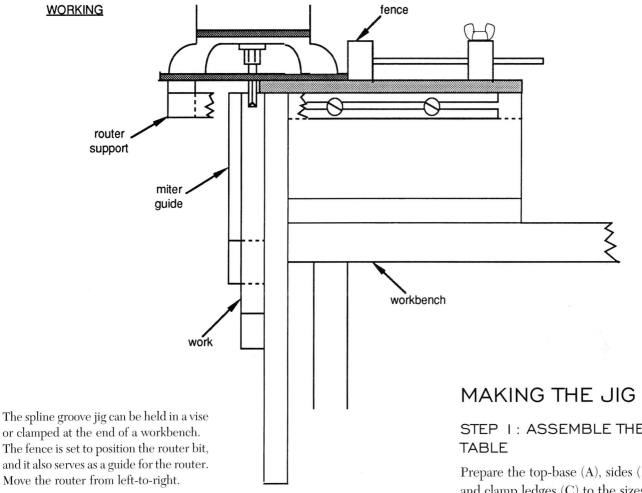

router
support

miter
guide

fence

work

workbench

The spline groove jig can be held in a vise or clamped at the end of a workbench. The fence is set to position the router bit, and it also serves as a guide for the router. Move the router from left-to-right.

QTY.	KEY	NAME	SIZE (IN INCHES)	MATERIAL
MATERIALS LIST				
SPLINE GROOVE JIG				
Base				
1	A	Top Base	$\frac{3}{4} \times 7\frac{1}{2} \times 11$	Plywood
2	B	Side	$\frac{3}{4} \times 4\frac{3}{4} \times 7\frac{1}{2}$	Plywood
2	C	Clamp Ledge	$\frac{3}{4} \times 2\frac{3}{8} \times 7\frac{1}{2}$	Plywood
1	D	Top	$\frac{1}{4} \times 8\frac{3}{8} \times 14$	Hardboard
1	E	Face	$\frac{3}{4} \times 12 \times 12\frac{1}{2}$	Plywood
1	F	Miter Guide	$1\frac{1}{2} \times 8\frac{3}{4} \times 12$	Pine

$\frac{3}{8}''$ Threaded Insert (1)

MAKING THE JIG

STEP 1: ASSEMBLE THE TABLE

Prepare the top-base (A), sides (B) and clamp ledges (C) to the sizes called for in the materials list. Form a $\frac{3}{8}''$-deep $\times$ $\frac{3}{4}''$-wide rabbet along one edge of the sides and add the clamp ledges to the sides with glue and 4d box nails. Attach the side/ledge-assemblies at the ends of the top-base with glue and 6d finishing nails.

Cut the face (E) to size and add it to the assembly with glue and 6d finishing nails. Drive the nails into the front edge of the top-base and the forward end of the sides.

Prepare the hardboard top (D) and install it on the top-base. Do this by applying glue to contact areas and holding the parts together with clamps, or by using contact cement. Be sure the top projects $\frac{3}{4}''$ at each side of the assembly and $\frac{1}{8}''$ beyond the face.

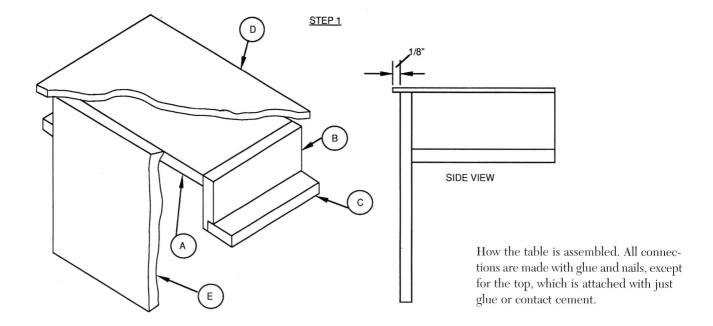

STEP 1

1/8"

SIDE VIEW

How the table is assembled. All connections are made with glue and nails, except for the top, which is attached with just glue or contact cement.

STEP 2

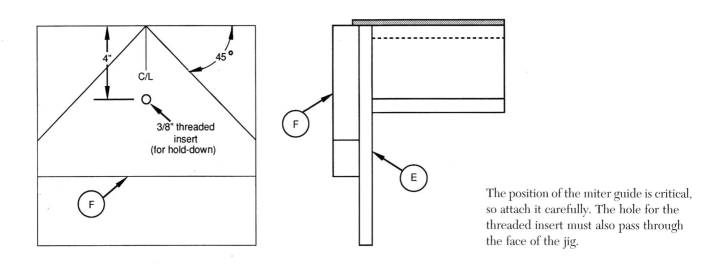

4"

45°

C/L

3/8" threaded insert (for hold-down)

The position of the miter guide is critical, so attach it carefully. The hole for the threaded insert must also pass through the face of the jig.

STEP 2: ADD THE MITER GUIDE

Cut the piece required for the miter guide (F) and draw an accurate centerline across its width. Use a right-angle template to mark the 45° lines. Saw a bit outside the lines and finish *to* the lines by sanding. Check with a combination square to be sure the cuts are accurate.

Drill the hole for the ⅜″ threaded insert that is needed for attaching a hold-down, and install the insert so it is a bit below the surface of the guide. The hole that you drill for the insert should also pass through the guide.

Position the guide carefully on the face of the jig and hold it there with clamps. Be sure the angle between the bearing edges of the guide and the projection of the jig's top is 45°. Attach the guide with three no.

8 × 1½″ flathead screws, to allow the guide to be replaced or readjusted, if necessary. Don't use glue.

STEP 3: MAKE THE FENCE

Prepare the pieces for the fence (G) and the support (H), and hold them together with clamps. Mark the locations of the holes that are needed for the bars and drill ¹⁄₁₆″ pilot holes. Enlarge the holes in what will be the

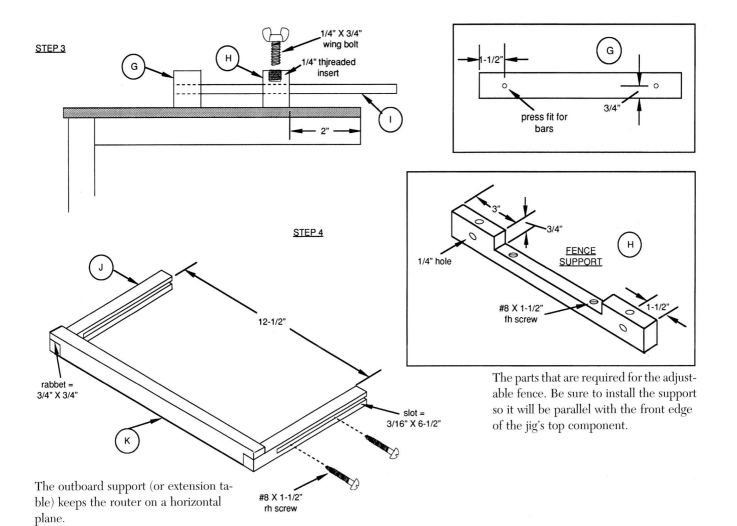

STEP 3

1/4" X 3/4" wing bolt

1/4" thjreaded insert

G

H

I

2"

1-1/2"

G

press fit for bars

3/4"

STEP 4

J

12-1/2"

rabbet = 3/4" X 3/4"

K

slot = 3/16" X 6-1/2"

#8 X 1-1/2" rh screw

3"

3/4"

1/4" hole

FENCE SUPPORT

H

#8 X 1-1/2" fh screw

1-1/2"

The parts that are required for the adjustable fence. Be sure to install the support so it will be parallel with the front edge of the jig's top component.

The outboard support (or extension table) keeps the router on a horizontal plane.

MATERIALS LIST				
SPLINE GROOVE JIG				
Fence Assembly				
QTY.	KEY	NAME	SIZE (IN INCHES)	MATERIAL
1	G	Fence	¾ × 1½ × 14	Hardwood
1	H	Support	¾ × 1½ × 14	Hardwood
2	I	Bars	¼ × 7	Steel Rod

¼″ Threaded Insert (2)

¼″ × ¾″ Wing Bolt (2)

No. 8 × 1½″ Flathead Screw (2)

OUTBOARD SUPPORT				
QTY.	KEY	NAME	SIZE (IN INCHES)	MATERIAL
2	J	Slide	¾ × ¾ × 8	Hardwood
1	K	Support	¾ × 1 × 14	Hardwood

No. 8 × 1½″ Round Head Screw (4)

support, to ¼″. Enlarge the holes in the fence to a bit less than ¼″ so the bars will fit tightly.

Make the layout for the notch in the support (see detail at top right) and saw the part to shape on a scroll saw or band saw. Drill the holes for the two ¼″ threaded inserts so they will be on line with the holes for the bars, and then install the inserts so they are flush with the top surface of the support.

Use a square to draw a line 2″ from the back edge of the jig's top. Hold the support on the line with a pair of clamps while you drill adequate holes for, and install the two no. 8 × 1½″ flathead screws that secure the support. Coat the ends of the bars with epoxy and tap them into place in the fence.

STEP 4: ASSEMBLE THE OUTBOARD SUPPORT

Cut the slides (J) to size and form the slots by drilling a ³⁄₁₆″ end-hole and sawing away the waste on a scroll saw or band saw.

Prepare the support (K) and form a ¾″-wide × ¾″-deep rabbet at each end. Apply glue to the contact areas of the slides and the support, and hold the parts together with clamps until the glue sets. It won't hurt to secure the joints with a no. 4 × ¾″ flathead screw.

STEP 5: SUPPLY THE HOLD-DOWN

Saw the part to size and, after rounding off its four corners, drill the ⅜″ hole for the wing bolt. Lay out the side profile and saw the part to shape on a scroll saw or band saw. It isn't critical for the profile to be exactly as drawn, as long as the ends are convex and the central area is thinned to ⅜″ or so.

The hold-down can be rotated so it is usable to secure either left- or right-hand miters.

USING THE JIG

To allow for the possibility of human error, identify one surface of each component, and place that surface against the face of the jig when forming the grooves. That way, the parts will still mesh even though the grooves might not be exactly centered.

Control the length of "blind" grooves by clamping strips of wood across the outboard support so they position the router for the beginning and end of the cut.

Splines can be made of hardboard or plywood. When made of wood, they will supply maximum strength if

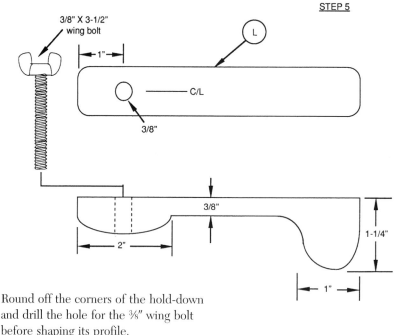

Round off the corners of the hold-down and drill the hole for the ⅜″ wing bolt before shaping its profile.

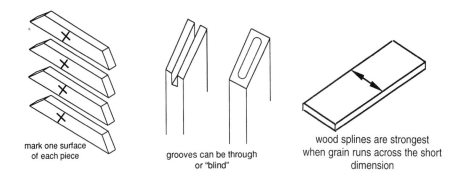

mark one surface of each piece

grooves can be through or "blind"

wood splines are strongest when grain runs across the short dimension

Spline "thoughts." Splines made of a contrasting material add a decorative detail to the joint.

MATERIALS LIST				
SPLINE GROOVE JIG **Hold-Down**				
QTY.	KEY	NAME	SIZE (IN INCHES)	MATERIAL
1	L	Bar	1⅛ × 1⅛ × 6	Hardwood
⅜″ × 3½″ Wing Bolt (1)				

the grain runs across the width of the part. Cut splines to the right width, but longer than necessary. Trim and sand them flush after the glue dries.

Portable Router Panel Routing Jig

The router follows the edge of the template or the jig itself. If the router feels unwieldy when it doesn't have the support of a template, place a piece of template material under the inboard edge of the router's base.

The panel routing jig is useful for a variety of template-guided routing operations. It's a practical accessory for forming inlay grooves in small projects and for creating decorative designs in cabinet doors and drawer fronts. The project is actually an adjustable frame that will accommodate square or rectangular components up to a maximum size of about 23" square.

MAKING THE JIG

STEP 1: MAKE THE BARS

Prepare the bars (A and B) by starting with 26"-long pieces of ¼" and ½" ply-wood of suitable width and then slicing off four 1⅜"-wide strips from each of them. Be careful when sawing, since the strips must have square ends and be of uniform width.

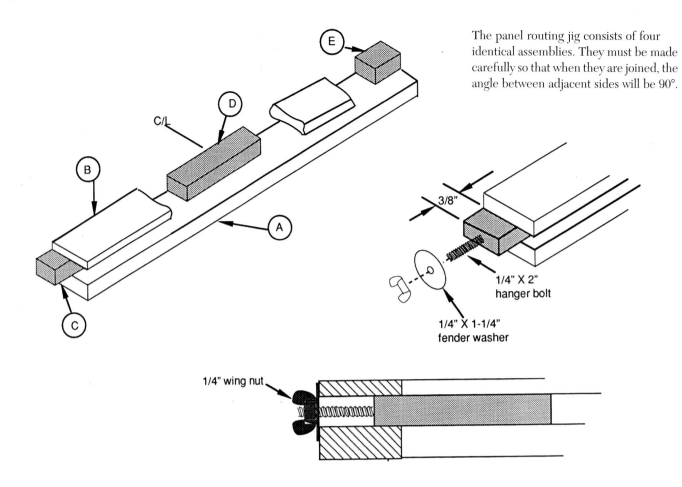

The panel routing jig consists of four identical assemblies. They must be made carefully so that when they are joined, the angle between adjacent sides will be 90°.

3/8"

1/4" X 2" hanger bolt

1/4" X 1-1/4" fender washer

1/4" wing nut

STEP 2: PREPARE THE SPACERS

All the spacers are ½"-thick and 1"-wide, so start with a long piece of stock with those dimensions, and saw off individual parts to the lengths shown in the materials list.

STEP 3: ASSEMBLY

Mark the locations of the spacers on the bottom bar. Spacer (D) is centered; (E) is flush at one end of the bar and (C) projects exactly ⅜" at the opposite end.

Apply glue to the contact areas of the spacers and bar and hold the parts together with small clamps. To speed up the job, you can drive 1" brads through the bar to hold the spacers so you don't have to wait for the glue to set.

Coat contact areas of the top bar and the spacers with glue and hold

the bar in place with clamps. Here too, you can use brads (¾") to maintain the bar's position.

Do the assembly work very carefully. The outside edges of the spacers and bars must be flush so the inside edge will have a ⅜"-deep "slot." Ends must be square, so that when the projection of spacer (C) is placed into the slot of an adjacent assembly, the angle between the components will be 90°.

MATERIALS LIST				
PANEL JIG				
QTY.	KEY	NAME	SIZE (IN INCHES)	MATERIAL
4	A	Bottom Bar	½ × 1⅜ × 26	Plywood
4	B	Top Bar	¼ × 1⅜ × 26	Plywood
4	C	Lock Spacer	½ × 1 × 3	Hardwood
4	D	Center Spacer	½ × 1 × 3	Hardwood
4	E	End Spacer	½ × 1 × 1	Hardwood
1/4-20 × 2" Hanger Bolt (4)			¼" × 1¼" Fender Washer (4)	
¼" Wing Nut (4)				

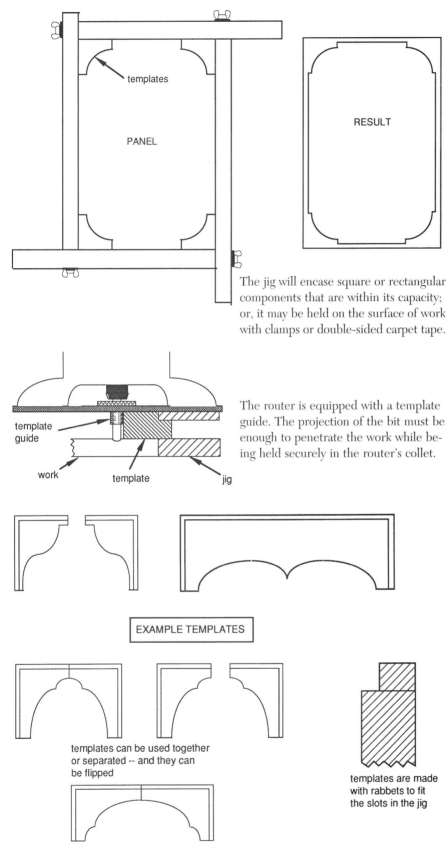

The jig will encase square or rectangular components that are within its capacity; or, it may be held on the surface of work with clamps or double-sided carpet tape.

The router is equipped with a template guide. The projection of the bit must be enough to penetrate the work while being held securely in the router's collet.

EXAMPLE TEMPLATES

templates can be used together or separated -- and they can be flipped

templates are made with rabbets to fit the slots in the jig

Templates can be any traditional or original design. Corner templates are rabbeted on two adjacent edges; full-length templates require rabbets on three edges. The rabbets are sized to provide a snug fit in the jig.

STEP 4: ADD THE HANGER BOLTS

Carefully mark the location of the hanger bolts at the center of spacer (C). Drill a ³⁄₁₆″ pilot hole before installing the bolts. The threaded portion of the hanger bolt must extend 1¼″ or so beyond the end of the spacer.

USING THE JIG

Adjust the jig to suit the size and shape of the work whenever possible as shown at top left. If the size of the work doesn't permit this, the jig can be held in place with clamps or double-sided carpet tape.

Routing is done with a template guide that follows lines established by the templates and, in some places, by the jig itself as shown at middle left. Sometimes on large projects, the weight of the router might cause some deflection on frame parts. Counter this by using pieces of ³⁄₈″ material in the slots, as shims, wherever they are needed. If you have made enough templates, idle ones can be used instead of shims.

A caution—when the work size makes it necessary to place the jig on the surface of the work instead of encasing it, you must use a router bit that is longer than the thickness of the jig in order to enter the work. Don't ever try to "extend" a bit's projection; it is imperative for the router's chuck to grip the bit securely.

The jig is designed for use with custom-made templates. Any traditional or original design can be used, as long as the templates are rabbeted on two or three edges so they will fit the slots in the jig as shown at bottom left. A good material to use for templates is medium-density fiberboard (MDF).

Portable Router Fluting Jig

One chore for the jig as a lathe is forming grooves on the circumference of the work. If the drill should prove unstable despite the keeper, brace the drill by placing a block of wood between it and the base of the jig. Keep the trigger depressed with a strip of tape.

Forming longitudinal grooves, like the examples in the drawing on page 131, on cylinders and squares is a pat chore for a portable router, as long as a jig that positions the work and guides the router is available. My prototype will accommodate components like legs for chairs, low tables and stands, but it can be easily modified to accept longer furniture parts. The design is essentially a U-shaped trough with a fixed "tailstock" and an adjustable "headstock." Vertically adjustable, improvised "centers" hold the work at each end; a fundamental indexing system allows the work to be rotated $x°$ for equally spaced cuts.

MAKING THE JIG

STEP 1: START WITH THE BASE (DETAIL "A")

Cut the base to width and length and mark it with a longitudinal centerline. Form a $\frac{1}{4}$"-deep × $\frac{1}{2}$"-wide groove about 8"-long down the center of the part, and then saw away a $\frac{3}{16}$"-wide strip down the center of the groove. The T-shaped slot that results is for the hex-head bolt that secures the position of the "headstock."

Next, form the ⅜″-deep × ¾″-wide rabbets on each edge of the base. Prepare the sides (B) and attach them to the base with glue and 5d box nails. Refer to the drawing on page 132.

STEP 2: ADD THE "TAILSTOCK" (DETAIL "B")

Cut part (C) to size, and form the centered slot by drilling a ¼″ end-hole and then removing the waste on a scroll saw or band saw. Form the ⅜″-deep × ¾″-wide rabbets on three sides, and install the part with glue and 5d box nails. It's a good idea to drill pilot holes through the hardwood before driving the nails.

STEP 3: ASSEMBLE THE "HEADSTOCK"

Cut part (D) to size, and form the ⅜″-deep × ¾″-wide rabbet along its bottom edge. Form the centered slot by following the procedure that was

The work is positioned in the jig so the spacing marks that are on it line up with the indexer. The indexing pin is tapped firmly into the end of the workpiece to keep it from rotating as cuts are made. Note the marks across the top edge of the sides of the jig. I use them to indicate where to stop moving the router.

suggested for the slot in the "tailstock."

Drill the four holes, locating them about ½″ away from the slot. Size the holes for a 6d or 7d box nail that will be used as an indexing pin.

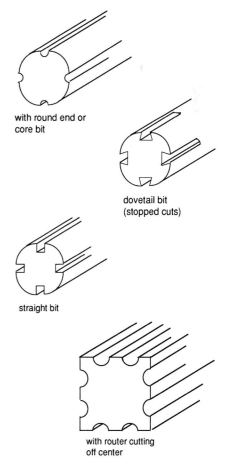

with round end or core bit

dovetail bit (stopped cuts)

straight bit

with router cutting off center

MATERIALS LIST				
ROUTER FLUTING JIG				
QTY.	KEY	NAME	SIZE (IN INCHES)	MATERIAL
1	A	Base	¾ × 5½ × 24	Pine
2	B	Side	¾ × 4⅛ × 24	Pine
1	C	Tailstock	¾ × 4½ × 5½	Pine
1	D	Headstock	¾ × 3¾ × 4	Hardwood
1	E	Headstock Base	¾ × 3⅜ × 4	Hardwood
1	F	Indexer	¹⁄₁₆ × 1 × 2½	Aluminum
1	G	Clamp Ledge	1 × 1½ × 5½	Hardwood

³⁄₁₆″ × 2″ Hex-Head Bolt with Washer and Nut (1)

¼″ × 2¼″ Threaded Rod (2)	¼″ Nut (4)
¼″ Wing Nut (2)	¼″ Washer (4)

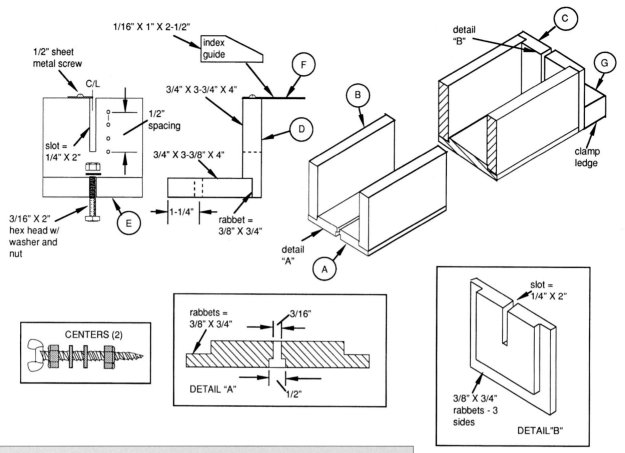

MATERIALS LIST				
DRILL AS A LATHE				
QTY.	KEY	NAME	SIZE (IN INCHES)	MATERIAL
1	A	Spur Center	⁵⁄₁₆	T-Nut
1	B	Shaft	⁵⁄₁₆ × 3½	Threaded Rod
1	C	Plate	¼ × 1½ × 4	Hardwood
		Drill Keeper	¾ × 4 × 7 (See Text)	Hardwood

⁵⁄₁₆″ Hex Nuts (3)

⁵⁄₁₆″ Fender Washers (2)

⁵⁄₁₆″ I.D. Bushing (1)

Prepare the base (E) and, after drilling the ³⁄₁₆″ centered hole, attach the two parts with glue and several no. 6 × 1½″ flathead screws.

Cut the index guide to the shape shown in the drawing. Put it in place on the "headstock," so its long edge is centered over the slot.

STEP 4: MAKE CENTERS

Use a hacksaw to cut two pieces of ¼″ threaded rod, 2¼″-long. Shape a point on the rods by chucking them in a drill press and working on them with a file. Attach the wing nuts by peening them onto the blunt end of the rods with a center punch.

AN OPTIONAL APPLICATION

I use the fluting jig occasionally as a drill-powered "lathe." This calls for a drive center and a custom-designed keeper for the drill. To make the keeper, start with a piece of hardwood with a width that fits between the sides of the jig, and longer than you might need. Mark the length of the part with a centerline and, allowing for about ¾″ edge-distance from the top of the part, use a hole saw or fly cutter to form a hole with a diameter to accommodate the section of the drill beyond the chuck.

Shape the keeper's top edge as shown in the drawing. Drill two pilot holes for the vertical screws and then make a saw-cut on the horizontal centerline of the hole. The length of the keeper must allow for some vertical adjustment of the drill. Secure the

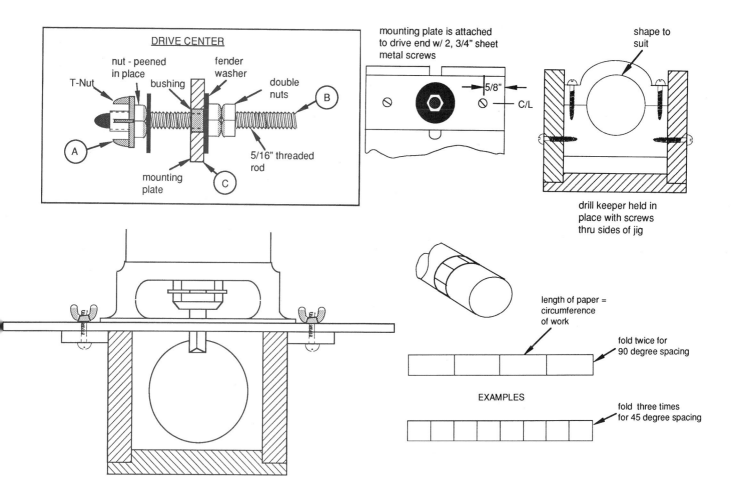

keeper with screws through the sides of the jig or—maybe a better idea—by using a small bar clamp. The latter idea eliminates having to drill holes, and provides a more flexible arrangement for vertical adjustment of the keeper.

MAKE THE DRIVE CENTER

Prepare the plate (C) and install the centered bushing by press-fitting it into an undersize hole. File a point on the end of the threaded rod. Secure the T-nut, which acts like a spur center, on the rod by peening a regular nut in place, or by using a lock nut.

The fender washers and the remaining nuts are installed as shown in the drawing. The mounting plate for the drive center is held against the "headstock" with screws or two small C-clamps.

USING THE JIG

INDEXING

Wrap a strip of paper around the work and cut it so its length equals the circumference of the piece. Fold the strip as needed to establish spacing of the cuts, and then put the paper back on the work and mark the fold lines.

Position the work in the jig by lining up the marks with the indexer. The work is held for the cut by tapping in the indexing pin.

WORKING

The router can be centered for the cut by using a commercial edge guide—or better still—with the special centering guide. The guide (described on page 120), provides better support for the router and can be adjusted for off-center cuts.

For all operations, put the work in place against the center in the "tailstock," and bring the "headstock" into position so the second center can bear against the opposite edge of the work. Be sure the work will be horizontal by placing a couple of small pieces of wood under the work as you tighten the centers.

Since both centers can be adjusted vertically, it's possible to have one lower than the other to allow tapering of the cuts. Tack-nail a strip of wood across the sides of the jig when you wish to make stopped cuts of equal length.

Cuts will be of optimum quality if you move the router slowly and perform deep cuts by making repeat passes. For the latter technique, make all the starting cuts, and then repeat them after increasing the projection of the router bit.

Router Master Jig

Accessories for the router master jig include a fence for straight-edge or field cuts, circular insert with a guide pin for pattern routing and an adjustable pivot guide for circular grooving. A plain insert and slide are in place when the special attachments are not being used.

Sometimes I think the perfect woodworking tool would be an extra pair of hands. Trying to hang onto the work and make accurate cuts while maneuvering a hand-held router is one scenario that comes to mind. Accuracy is important, because I use my router for everything from shaping woodworking joints to fashioning decorative silhouettes. My solution: a jig that turned my router into a versatile stationary tool, capable of most of the chores I relegate to the tool (see drawing on page 136).

Some woodworkers refer to my portable router master jig as an "overarm router." I don't mind, especially since commercial overarm routers, which have an integral power head, can cost almost more than my entire shop—and for negligible cost, you can have the master jig that operates with a router you probably already have on hand.

The current version of the master jig evolved from several prototypes—the most successful of which had the

The jig makes tricky tasks—like forming edge dovetail grooves—routine. For accuracy, be sure the edges of the work are square to adjacent surfaces to begin with. Keep the work firmly against the fence throughout the pass.

To make a matching "tongue" for the dovetail, keep the carriage at the same height, but adjust the fence to cut on the outside edge of the material. The first pass shapes one side. The second side is shaped by turning the stock end-for-end.

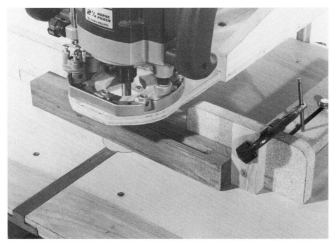

Control the length of mortises by clamping a block of wood to the fence to serve as a stop. Mark the fence so the work can be placed for the start of the cut. The position of the fence determines whether the mortise will be on or off the center of the work.

When forming rabbets, the fence position determines the width of the cut; the height of the cutter above the table determines its depth. The work area is amply covered by the carriage so there's no need for hands to come close to the danger zone.

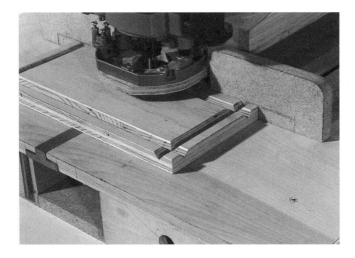

The fence also ensures edge-distance accuracy when surface grooving in the field. On chores like this, and when rabbeting or shaping on adjacent edges, make the cross-grain cuts first. The final with-the-grain cuts will remove the imperfections that inevitably occur at the ends of cross-grain cuts.

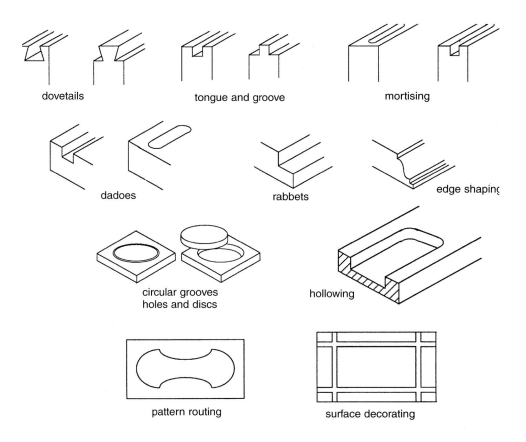

dovetails

tongue and groove

mortising

dadoes

rabbets

edge shaping

circular grooves
holes and discs

hollowing

pattern routing

surface decorating

router on a shelf that was adjustable vertically on a 2″-diameter heavy steel tube. But readers commented (complained) that they couldn't find a similar piece of steel tube. So, what I have in my shop now is the same concept, but with the router on a carriage that moves on twin tubes of the type readily available at home supply centers.

Because of the carriage, the router loses some depth-of-cut, but when the original capacity is 2″ or more, losing a half-inch isn't critical, even when forming mortises. I use a plunge router with the jig so I can preset depth of cut and, also, it's easy to duplicate cuts of similar depth.

The project isn't difficult to make, but it has some key details that call for extra care. It's a good idea to have the router you plan to use (preferably a "middleweight") and the twin tubes on hand before sizing components.

MAKING THE JIG

STEP 1: START WITH THE SUBSTRUCTURE

Saw the base to size and mark a centerline across its width; then mark the locations of the two partitions (C) and the sides (B). Before going further, refer to the drawing at bottom left

MATERIALS LIST				
ROUTER MASTER JIG				
Substructure				
QTY.	KEY	NAME	SIZE (IN INCHES)	MATERIAL
1	A	Base	¾ × 23 × 28¾	Plywood
2	B	Sides	¾ × 3½ × 23	Plywood
2	C	Partition	¾ × 3½ × 22¼	Plywood
Top				
QTY.	KEY	NAME	SIZE (IN INCHES)	MATERIAL
1	A	Top	¾ × 23½ × 30	Plywood
1	B	Slide Support	¾ × 5 × 10	Pine
5⁄16″ Threaded Insert (5)			5⁄16″ × 1″ Wing Bolt (1)	
No. 12 × 1½″ Flathead Screw (12)				

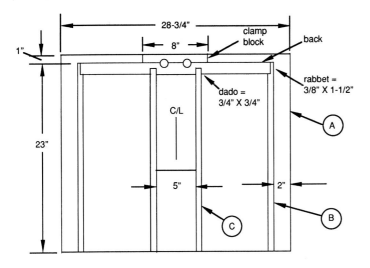

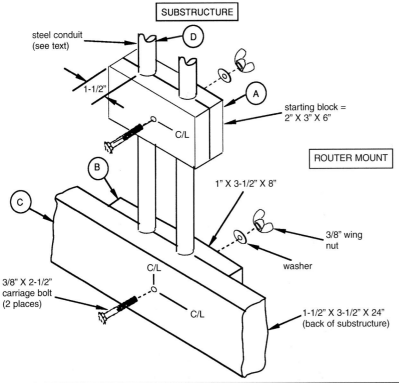

MATERIALS LIST				
ROUTER MASTER JIG				
Router Mount				
QTY.	KEY	NAME	SIZE (IN INCHES)	MATERIAL
1	A	Clamp Block	$2 \times 3 \times 6$	Hardwood
2	B	Clamp	$1 \times 3\frac{1}{2} \times 8$	Hardwood
1	C	Back Of Sub-structure	$1\frac{1}{2} \times 3\frac{1}{2} \times 24$	Hardwood
2	D	Conduit	(See Text)	Steel
$\frac{3}{8}'' \times 2\frac{1}{2}''$ Carriage Bolt with Nut and Washer (1)				

(router mount) which shows the relationship between the back of the substructure (C) and the clamp (B). Prepare both parts, and mark a centerline across the top edge of each of them.

Form the two $\frac{3}{4}'' \times \frac{3}{4}''$ dadoes in the back that will receive the partitions. Be sure the dadoes are located so the distance between the partitions will be 5″. Clamp the clamp block to the back so it is centered and then, from the centerlines, carefully mark the 3″ O.C. location of the tubes.

Work carefully on a drill press to bore the holes for the tubes on the joint line of the two components. The outside diameter of the tubes is a bit less than $\frac{15}{16}''$, so a $\frac{7}{8}''$-diameter hole should provide enough bearing against the tubes when the parts are joined. If you find that the tubes will not be held securely, decrease the thickness of the clamp block a bit by sanding its face. Drill the hole for the $\frac{3}{8}''$ carriage bolt while the parts are still clamped together, and then separate the two pieces.

STEP 2: RETURN TO THE SUBSTRUCTURE

Form the $\frac{3}{8}''$-deep $\times 1\frac{1}{2}''$-wide rabbets on the end of the sides and join them to the back with glue and 4d box nails. Apply glue to the bottom edges of the assembly and carefully clamp it to the base. Be sure the angle between the back and sides is 90° and that the sides are parallel with the edges of the base. Drive 6d finishing nails up through the base into the edges of the sides and back.

Prepare the partitions and, after coating contact areas with glue, hold them in correct position with clamps. Here too, drive 6d finishing nails up through the base into the edges of the partitions.

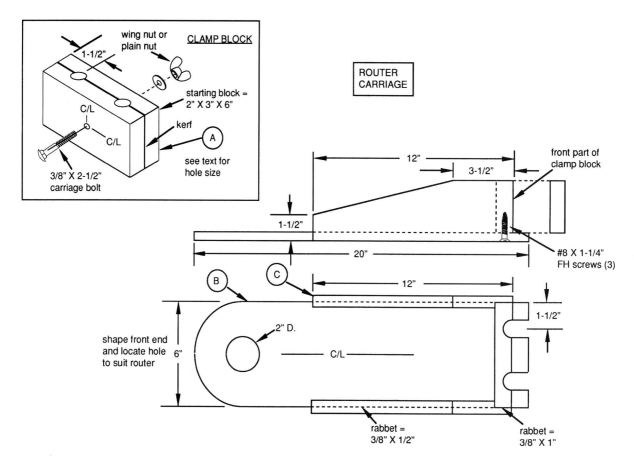

MATERIALS LIST				
ROUTER MASTER JIG				
Router Carriage				
QTY.	KEY	NAME	SIZE (IN INCHES)	MATERIAL
1	A	Clamp Block	2 × 3 × 6	Hardwood
1	B	Shelf	½ × 6 × 20	Plywood
2	C	Sides	¾ × 3½ × 12	Pine
No. 8 × 1¼″ Flathead Screws (3)			⅜″ × 2½″ Carriage Bolt with Nut and Washer (1)	

STEP 3: ASSEMBLE THE ROUTER CARRIAGE

We go to the router carriage at this point because the position of the router will have a bearing on some factors affecting the top of the base.

Start with the clamp block (detail above). Prepare the part and mark its top edge with a lengthwise centerline. Mark the location of the holes for the tubes on the centerline, and work on a drill press with a Forstner bit or brad-point bit to bore the ⅞″ holes. Drill the hole for the ⅜″ carriage bolt and then "split" the block on the centerline by sawing on a band saw.

Next, cut the shelf (B) to size and shape its front end to suit the router. Bore the access hole for router bits and, using the router's subbase as a template, drill holes for the attach-ment screws. Because the shelf is ½″-thick you'll probably have to substitute flathead screws that are longer than the original ones.

Notice that the back end of the shelf is notched to fit the tubes. Form the notches by boring ⅞″ end-holes and then sawing away the waste.

Position the front part of the clamp block on the shelf and, after applying glue to contact areas, hold it in place with a clamp while you drive three no. 8 × 1¼″ flathead screws up through the bottom of the shelf.

Cut the sides (C) to size and shape and then form the ⅜″-deep × ½″-wide rabbet along the bottom edges, and the ⅜″-deep × 1″-wide rabbet on the rear edges. Use glue on contact areas and hold the sides in place with clamps. Be sure that the angle between the shelf and the clamp block is 90°. Drive 3d finishing nails through the sides into the shelf and the clamp block.

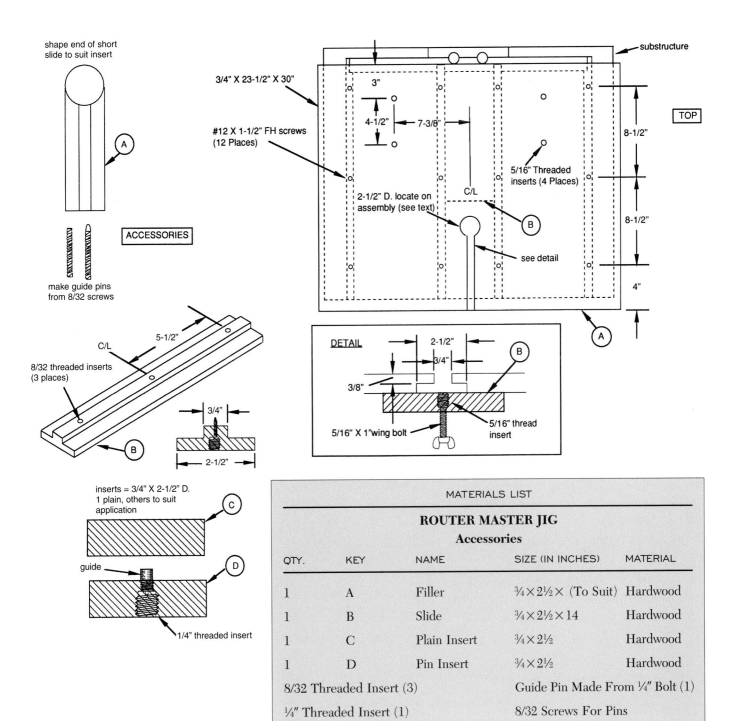

shape end of short
slide to suit insert

A

ACCESSORIES

make guide pins
from 8/32 screws

3/4" X 23-1/2" X 30"

#12 X 1-1/2" FH screws
(12 Places)

substructure

TOP

3"

4-1/2" 7-3/8"

5/16" Threaded
inserts (4 Places)

2-1/2" D. locate on
assembly (see text)

C/L

B

see detail

8-1/2"

8-1/2"

4"

A

5-1/2"

C/L

8/32 threaded inserts
(3 places)

B

3/4"

2-1/2"

DETAIL

2-1/2"

3/4"

3/8"

B

5/16" X 1"wing bolt

5/16" thread
insert

inserts = 3/4" X 2-1/2" D.
1 plain, others to suit
application

C

guide

D

1/4" threaded insert

QTY.	KEY	NAME	SIZE (IN INCHES)	MATERIAL
		MATERIALS LIST		
		ROUTER MASTER JIG		
		Accessories		
1	A	Filler	¾ × 2½ × (To Suit)	Hardwood
1	B	Slide	¾ × 2½ × 14	Hardwood
1	C	Plain Insert	¾ × 2½	Hardwood
1	D	Pin Insert	¾ × 2½	Hardwood
8/32 Threaded Insert (3)			Guide Pin Made From ¼″ Bolt (1)	
¼″ Threaded Insert (1)			8/32 Screws For Pins	

Secure the tubes in the base's clamp arrangement and, after mounting the router on the shelf, put the carriage in place on the tubes. If you find that you can't bear sufficiently against the tubes by using the thumb screws, substitute hex nuts so you can do the tightening with a wrench.

STEP 4: NOW TO THE TOP OF THE BASE

Saw the top to size and draw a centerline across its width. Mark the location of the four ⁵⁄₁₆″ threaded inserts that are needed for the bolts that will secure the fence. Install the inserts so they will be a bit lower than the surface of the top.

Put the top in position and hold it there with clamps. Place a small round-end bit in the router and lower the bit to mark a point on the top's centerline. With the mark as a center, use a fly cutter or a hole saw to form a 2½″-diameter hole through the top.

STEP 5: FORM THE T-SLOT

Referring to the drawing at the top of page 139, form the T-slot by first using a dadoing tool to shape a ⅜"-deep × 2½"-wide groove that ends at the hole in the top, and then sawing away a ¾"-wide center strip. It's important that the T-slot runs exactly on the centerline of the top.

Cut the support (B) to size and, after installing the 5⁄16" threaded insert an inch or so from its front edge, attach the support to the underside of the top with glue and 4d box nails. Here too, be sure the support is centered and that it fits nicely between the base's partitions.

STEP 6: PUT THE TOP IN PLACE

Locate the top very carefully on the substructure and hold it there with a pair of clamps. Mark the location of the attachment screws, and drill adequate countersunk holes for the no. 8 × 1½" flathead screws. Remove the top so you can clean away waste and, after coating the top edges of the substructure components with glue, replace the top and secure it with the twelve screws.

The pivot slide is used for accurate circular grooving. The greater radius is measured from the center of the pivot point to the outside of the cutter. Use the blunt or pointed pivot point depending on whether the work has or does not have a center hole. If you plan to route a disc, place a piece of scrap over the pivot and attach the work to the scrap with strips of double-faced tape.

For pattern routing, use the insert that has the guide pin (arrow). Work with a router bit with a diameter to match that of the guide pin. A pattern, or template, is tack-nailed to the underside of the workpiece. The height of the guide pin above the table should be less than the thickness of the pattern.

Moving the work so that the pattern bears constantly against the guide pin allows the cutter to duplicate the shape of the pattern. It helps to practice how to move the work a few times before bringing the router bit into play. You can make several inserts, each with a different pin diameter, so you can be more flexible about choosing a bit of particular diameter.

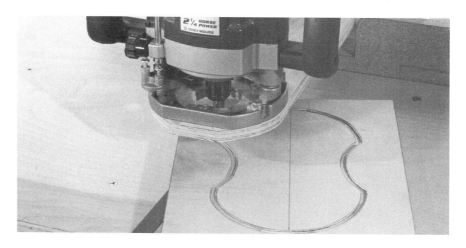

STEP 7: PREPARE SLIDES AND INSERTS

The slides (A and B) are similar, so it's best to start by producing the cross-section shape on a long piece of stock and sawing it into individual pieces. Be sure to use a pusher to get the work past the cutter when forming the edge rabbets. Shape one end of slide (A), used as a filler, to suit the hole in the top, and then saw it to suitable length.

Drill the holes in slide (B) for the 8/32 threaded inserts and install the inserts so they will be flush with the bottom of the slide.

Make the guide pins by removing the head from 8/32 screws. Leave one blunt; shape a point on the other by chucking it in the drill press and working on it with a file. Alternately, grip the screw in a portable drill and spin it against a turning grinding wheel.

Use a fly cutter to form the inserts so you can size them to fit snugly in the hole in the top of the base. One insert, used as a filler, is plain. The other insert, for pattern routing, is equipped with a centered ¼″ threaded insert for a guide that is made from a ¼″ machine screw.

STEP 8: ASSEMBLE THE FENCE

Cut the face (A) to size and then mark it to indicate the centered cutout and the notches in the base that will receive the guide (B). The profile of the part can be produced entirely on a scroll saw or band saw but it is more efficient to form the notches by making repeat passes with a dadoing tool. However you work, size the notches so they will provide a snug fit for the guides.

Cut the guides to size, and form the centered slot by drilling a ⁵⁄₁₆″ end-hole and cleaning out the waste

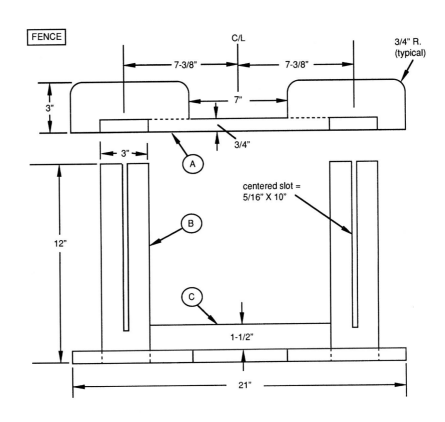

by sawing on a scroll saw or band saw.

Put the guides in place with glue and 6d finishing nails, driving the nails up through the bottom of the guides.

Size the stiffener (C) so it will fit nicely between the guides and against the face. Use only glue to install the stiffener.

MATERIALS LIST				
ROUTER MASTER JIG				
Fence				
QTY.	KEY	NAME	SIZE (IN INCHES)	MATERIAL
1	A	Face	¾ × 3 × 21	MDF
1	B	Guides	¾ × 3 × 11¼	MDF
1	C	Stiffener	¾ × 1½ × 11¾	MDF
⁵⁄₁₆″ × 1¼″ Bolt and Washer (4)				
Drawer				
QTY.	KEY	NAME	SIZE (IN INCHES)	MATERIAL
2	A	Bottom	¼ × 8¼ × 20	Plywood
4	B	Side	½ × 3 × 20	Plywood
2	C	Back	¾ × 3 × 7¼	Pine
2	D	Front	¾ × 3½ × 8¾	Plywood

STEP 9: MAKE THE DRAWERS

The drawers are straightforward; nothing fancy, but adequate for the purpose. Check the opening in the base that will receive the drawers before cutting components, just in case some modifying is in order. Prepare the bottom and the sides, and assemble them with glue and 3d finishing nails. Cut the back to fit, and put in place with glue and 3d finishing nails up through the bottom and 6d finishing nails through the sides.

Prepare the front, and after forming the rabbets at both ends and the bottom, bore a centered, 1″ finger hole through it. Attach the front with glue and then drive a few 3d finishing nails up through the bottom and 4d finishing nails through the sides.

STEP 10: ANTI-DEFLECTOR

The anti-deflector is optional, but it's a good thought, especially if you use a heavy router. If the carriage does tilt a bit downward, it will most likely occur if the carriage position is high on the tubes when forming a shape on the edge of a wide piece of stock.

Anyway, the unit can be added at a later date when an operation indicates that it might be needed. The drawing suggests two options—the plain steel rod with sliding collar would be the easiest to adjust; but in either case, do not attach the block in which the rod—plain or threaded—seats.

USING THE JIG

The photographs demonstrate some of the chores that can be accomplished with the router master jig. It's always best to situate the router as close to the work as possible. Don't force cuts; allow the bit to work at its own pace. When deep cuts are needed, mortising for example, get to the final result by making repeat passes. When forming a shape on the edge of a workpiece, be sure from the beginning that the edges of the part are square to adjacent surfaces.

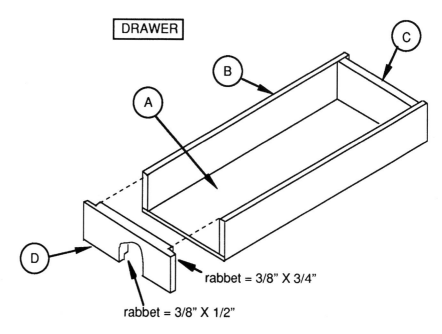

DRAWER

rabbet = 3/8" X 3/4"

rabbet = 3/8" X 1/2"

OPTIONAL "ANTI-DEFLECTOR"

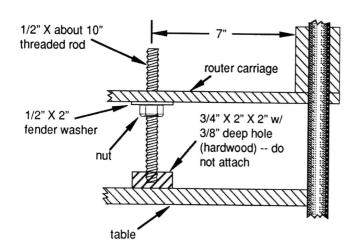

1/2" X about 10" threaded rod

7"

router carriage

1/2" X 2" fender washer

3/4" X 2" X 2" w/ 3/8" deep hole (hardwood) -- do not attach

nut

table

ALTERNATE METHOD

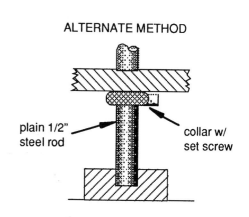

plain 1/2" steel rod

collar w/ set screw

Miter Saw Work Station

M iter saws are fine tools, but even the best of them—including those equipped with extensions—don't provide adequate support surface for the jobs they are designed for. My favorite lumber yard has one set up on a sturdy stand with fixed wings so it can easily and safely support a 12′, or longer, 2 × 4. That's fine for a barn-size workshop, but when I thought about a similar setup for myself, I had to consider space limitations. It didn't take a brainstorm to see a special stand with hinged extensions so that, when idle, the project wouldn't need more space than the tool itself. Since customizing was in order, it followed that other features could be added—like a stop that's usable on either side of the saw, a storage drawer and an accessory that makes it easier to produce accurate compound cuts.

The size of the unit is suitable for almost any saw—those I've examined anyway—but you might check the width of your machine and, if necessary, change the width of the stand's top. It should be wide enough to accommodate the saw plus the two short extensions that are permanently attached to it.

CONSTRUCTION

STEP 1: PREPARE STAND COMPONENTS

Start by cutting the legs, the three longer rails, and the four side rails, to the lengths called for in the materials

When idle, the miter saw work station doesn't need much more space than the saw itself. The fixed extensions add work support when short stock is worked on. The drawer offers generous storage for small tools or accessories. You can add casters to the stand, but be sure they have a locking feature. The stop will function on either side of the saw and it can be inverted when necessary.

Work support increases to about 5' when one extension is used. Support increases to more than 7½' when both extensions are up.

list. All the rails have a rabbet cut at each end that is ¾"-deep × 1½"-wide. The rabbets can be formed with a dado-assembly, but results will be better—smoother—if you work with a tenoning jig. Saw the shoulder cuts first, working in normal crosscut position, then use the jig to make the cheek cuts.

STEP 2: ASSEMBLE THE STAND

Start assembly by applying glue to the rabbet cuts in the side rails and holding them in place against the legs with clamps. Then drill for and install the no. 10 × 1½" flathead screws. Before going further, attach the drawer rail (D) to the inside of the legs with glue and 6d finishing nails.

Next, add the two rear rails and the front one, again after coating the rabbet cuts with glue. While the assembly is "open," install the two top drawer rails (E). Glue alone is enough here if you keep the parts in place with clamps, but you can toe-nail through the top of the guides into

the legs if you wish. The purpose of the top rails is to keep the drawer from tilting when you pull it out.

The final step for the substructure is to cut the shelf to overall size, and then notch it at the two back corners so it will fit the rear legs. Attach the shelf with glue and 6d nails.

The top for the stand has a ⅜"-deep × ¾"-wide groove running

across its length. The forward shoulder of the groove must align with the bearing surface of the tool's fences, so place the tool on the stand and check for correct position before you form the groove. Attach the top with no. 10 × 1½" flathead screws and then, with the tool centered, drill the holes that are needed to bolt the tool in place.

MATERIALS LIST				
MITER SAW WORK STATION				
Miter Saw Stand				
QTY.	KEY	NAME	SIZE (IN INCHES)	MATERIAL
4	A	Leg	1½ × 3½ × 31¼	Clear Fir
3	B	Rail	1½ × 3½ × 22½	Clear Fir
4	C	Side Rail	1½ × 3½ × 12	Clear Fir
2	D	Drawer Rail	¾ × 1½ × 15¼	Clear Fir
2	E	Drawer Rail	¾ × 1½ × 14½	Clear Fir
1	F	Shelf	¾ × 13¼ × 24	Plywood
1	G	Top	¾ × 18 × 29	Plywood

No. 10 × 1½" Flathead Screw (36)

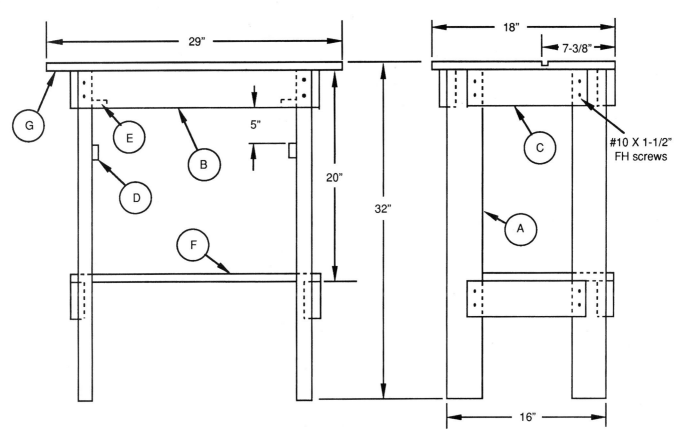

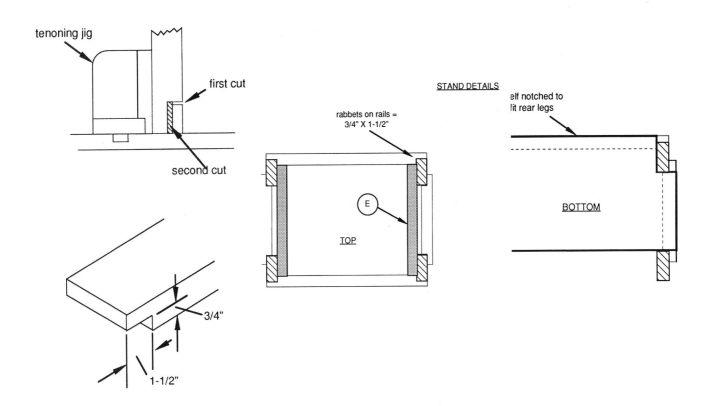

STAND DETAILS

tenoning jig

first cut

second cut

3/4"

1-1/2"

rabbets on rails =
3/4" X 1-1/2"

TOP

elf notched to
fit rear legs

BOTTOM

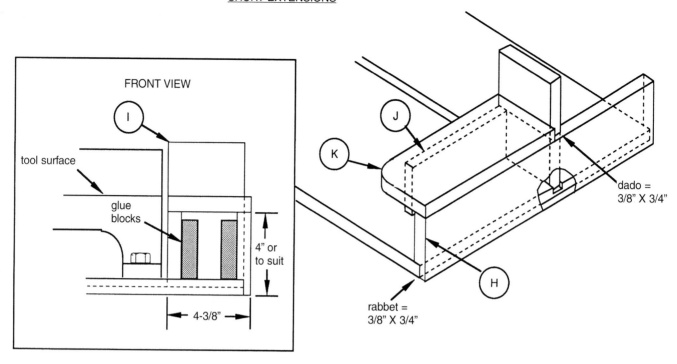

FRONT VIEW

tool surface

glue blocks

4" or to suit

4-3/8"

dado = 3/8" X 3/4"

rabbet = 3/8" X 3/4"

MATERIALS LIST

MITER SAW WORK STATION
Short Extensions

QTY.	KEY	NAME	SIZE (IN INCHES)	MATERIAL
2	H	End Piece	¾ × 4 × 18	Pine
2	I	Fence	¾ × 4 × 7	Pine
2	J	Support	¾ × 3¼ × 8½	Pine
2	K	Table	¾ × 4⅜ × 10⅝	Pine

Folding Extensions

QTY.	KEY	NAME	SIZE (IN INCHES)	MATERIAL
2	L	Table	¾ × 10½ × 29	Plywood
2	M	Trim	½ × ¾ × 10½	Fir
2	N	Trim	½ × ¾ × 29	Fir
2	O	Fence	¾ × 3¾ × 29	Fir
2	P	Top Brace	1 × 1½ × 14	Fir
2	Q	Bottom Brace	1 × 1½ × 20	Fir
2	R	Piano Hinge	1 × 1 × 10½	
2	S	Backflap Hinge	1½ × 1½ × 2	

⅜" Threaded Insert (2)   Screws for Hinges

⅜" × 2" Wing Bolt (2)

STEP 3: ADD THE SHORT EXTENSIONS

The materials list offers dimensions for the components that comprise the short extensions, but they should be checked against the tool's position and the height of its table. Start by preparing the end piece, making sure that its height above the top of the stand equals that of the tool's table *less ¾"*. Form the rabbet at the bottom edge of the end piece and then the dado which should mate with the groove in the stand's top. Attach the component with glue and 4d box nails.

The fence (I), which fits in the groove in the stand's top and in the dado in the end piece, is secured with glue and 4d box nails. Cut the support short enough so it won't interfere with a full swing of the tool's indexing handle. Put the support in place with glue and 4d box nails, and then add the glue blocks to strengthen the assembly. Last step is to add the table (K) with glue and 6d finishing nails.

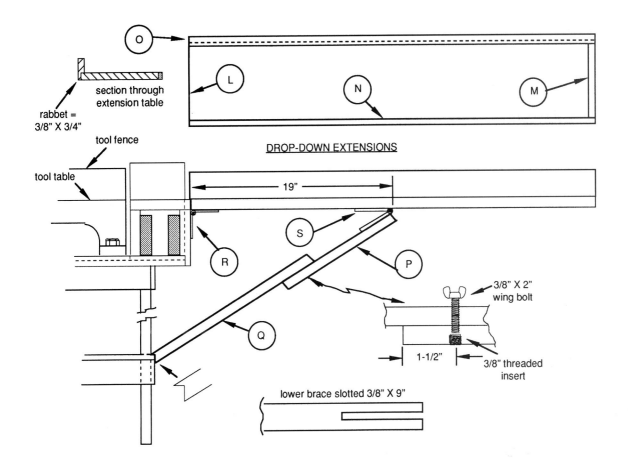

section through
extension table

rabbet =
3/8" X 3/4"

tool fence

tool table

O

L

N

M

DROP-DOWN EXTENSIONS

19"

S

R

P

Q

3/8" X 2"
wing bolt

1-1/2"

3/8" threaded
insert

lower brace slotted 3/8" X 9"

When forming the components for the short extensions, remember that the assemblies are *left* and *right*.

STEP 4: THE DROP-DOWN EXTENSIONS

When you start assembly of the drop-down extensions, remember that, like the short extensions, they are *left* and *right*. Cut the tables to size and then add the trim strips with glue and 6d finishing nails. Form the ⅜"-deep × ¾"-wide rabbet along the bottom edge of the fence, and add it to the table with glue and 5d box nails. Be sure the angle between fence and table is 90°.

STEP 5: ATTACHING THE EXTENSIONS

Follow this procedure to be sure the fences of the project will be accurately aligned: Remove the tool from

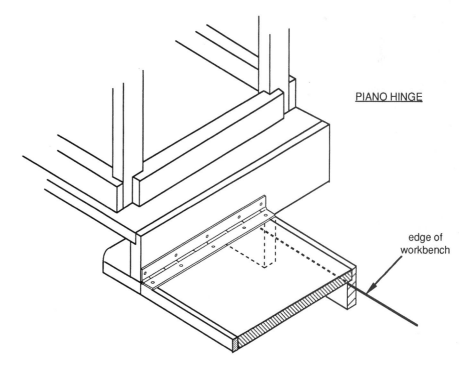

PIANO HINGE

edge of
workbench

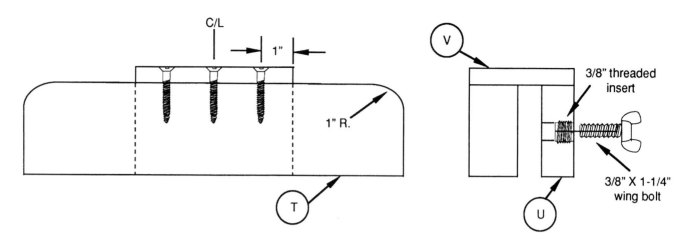

STOP

DRAWER

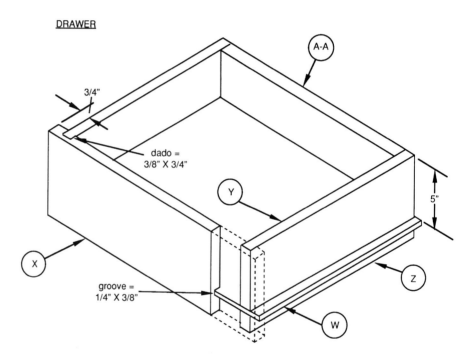

the stand. Invert the stand and place it on the workbench so the fence of the short extensions butt against the edge of the workbench. Place the drop-down extension so *its* fence also butts against the workbench edge, and use a clamp to keep the component in position.

Install the piano hinge and then add the backflap hinge. The project can remain in this position while you prepare the braces. Make the top one first and, after installing the ⅜″ threaded insert, attach it to the back-flap hinge. The bottom brace is slotted at one end and shaped at the other so it can rest solidly against the stand's shelf. The slot is needed for table-level adjustment and to allow braces to be "folded" out of the way when the extensions are lowered. Details for the braces are shown in in the drawing at the top of page 147.

STEP 6: MAKE THE STOP

The stop is designed so it will function on either extension and it can be inverted when necessary. Cut all parts to size, but adjust the width of the top (V) so the gap between the front and back will be ¾″ plus about ¹⁄₃₂″. Install the ⅜″ threaded insert in the back component, and then as-

semble the pieces with glue and no. 10 × 1¼″ flathead screws.

STEP 7: CONSTRUCT THE DRAWER

The drawer design isn't fancy, but the unit is sturdy and suits the purpose. Start with the bottom, making sure that it slides smoothly between the legs of the stand. Cut the front to size, form the groove for the bottom and the dadoes for the sides. Prepare the

sides, and then assemble the four pieces with glue and finishing nails. The guides are installed in line with the sides, but before attaching them permanently, check to see that they will slide smoothly along the drawer rails in the stand. Finally, use glue and 6d finishing nails to install the back. The extension of the front below the bottom of the drawer provides for pulling the unit out, so a handle isn't needed.

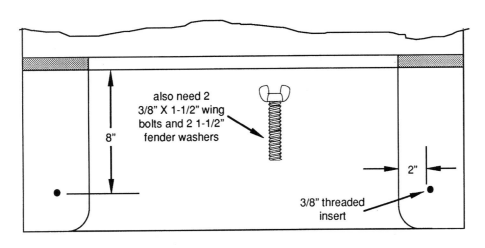

OPTIONAL HOLD-IN
also need 2
3/8" X 1-1/2" wing
bolts and 2 1-1/2"
fender washers
8"
2"
3/8" threaded
insert
4"
3/4" X 9" X 29"
slot =
3/8" X 5"
1-1/2" R.
(typical)

MATERIALS LIST

MITER SAW WORK STATION

Stop

QTY.	KEY	NAME	SIZE (IN INCHES)	MATERIAL
1	T	Front	$1\frac{1}{2} \times 2\frac{3}{4} \times 12$	Clear Fir
1	U	Back	$1 \times 2\frac{3}{4} \times 5$	Clear Fir
1	V	Top	$\frac{1}{2} \times 3\frac{1}{2}$ $(+\frac{1}{32}) \times 5$	Clear Fir

No. 10 × 1¼″ Flathead Screw (6)

⅜″ Threaded Insert (1)

⅜″ × 1¼″ Wing Bolt (1)

Drawer

QTY.	KEY	NAME	SIZE (IN INCHES)	MATERIAL
1	W	Bottom	$\frac{1}{4} \times 15 \times 19\frac{1}{2}$	Plywood
1	X	Front	$\frac{3}{4} \times 6\frac{1}{2} \times 19\frac{1}{2}$	Plywood
2	Y	Side	$\frac{3}{4} \times 4\frac{3}{4} \times 15$	Plywood
2	Z	Guide	$\frac{3}{4} \times 1\frac{1}{4} \times 15$	Fir
1	A-A	Back	$\frac{3}{4} \times 4\frac{3}{4} \times 16\frac{1}{2}$	Plywood

STEP 8: PREPARE THE HOLD-IN

The hold-in isn't essential for the project's normal functions, but you'll find it very handy when doing chores like compound sawing. Its purpose is to act as a brace so work can be held at a slope angle against the fence. For example, if the saw is set for a 45° miter, the result will be a correct compound cut regardless of the work's slope angle. Even if your saw can be tilted for bevel cuts, the hold-in is desirable since it eliminates one critical compound angle setting.

The accessory calls for installing two ⅜″ threaded inserts in the tables of the short extensions, locating them as shown in above. Cut the hold-in to overall size, and form the slots by drilling ⅜″ end-holes and sawing away the waste. Produce the final shape on a scroll saw or band saw. Smooth the sawed edges by sanding.

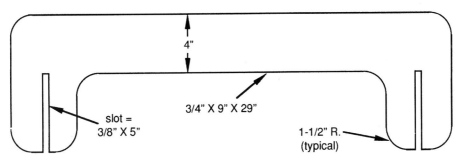

Portable Circular Saw, Crosscut and Miter Jig

The crosscut and miter jig for a portable saw has enough capacity between its fences for some amount of gang cutting. Here, I'm crosscutting three pieces of 2×4. The saw will move smoothly if you coat the bearing edges of the track occasionally with paste wax or a dry lubricant.

The crosscut and miter jig for a portable circular saw provides for accurate sawing, whether it's used in the shop, on the workbench or in the field, supported by a pair of sawhorses. There are commercial guides for portable saws, but with them, there is the problem of using one hand to secure the guide and the other hand to manipulate the saw. And there is the further nuisance of having to keep the workpiece secure.

The project provides ample support for the work; the saw-bearing track adjusts for crosscutting and angular cuts up to 45°. The jig's capacity is for stock 1½″ or less in thickness; the distance between its fences allows sawing lumber or plywood up to about 12″-wide.

The distance between the arms of the track must suit the tool you will use. Other jig dimensions should be right for just about any saw.

MAKING THE JIG

STEP 1: START WITH THE BASE AND FENCES

Cut the base and the fences to size and mark each piece with a centerline. Since the thickness of 2×4 material can vary somewhat, it's necessary that the fences be thick enough to accommodate any variation. You can plane down thicker stock to 1⅜", or "veneer" the fences with ⅛"-thick plywood or hardboard. If you opt for veneering, cut the risers oversize and, after attaching them with contact cement, trim them to match the length and width of the fences.

Install the ⅜" threaded insert on the centerline of the rear fence (C). Coat contact areas of the fences and the base with glue and hold the fences in place with clamps while you drive the no. 10×1¾" flathead screws up through the bottom of the base. The stops (E), shown on page 152, are installed after the track is made.

STEP 2: ASSEMBLE THE TRACK

Prepare the supports (F) and the arms (G). Locate the position of the arms by drawing lines across the supports 4" away from each end. Apply glue to mating pieces and keep the parts in place with clamps while you drive 1" brads up through the supports. You can opt to use no. 6×1" flathead screws in place of brads.

Next, cut the ends (H) to size and install them with glue and brads or screws. Be sure when adding the end pieces that the arm assemblies are parallel and that their bearing edges are square to the end pieces. Last assembly step is to add the fillers (I). Secure them with glue and brads or screws.

I use the jig for sawing lumber or plywood, in addition to structural material. Making a 45° cut on 12"-wide stock is easier with the jig than it would be when using a table saw.

The lock pins are used to position the track for crosscutting and 45° angular positions. Other pin locations can be added when needed. The projection of the pin above the track must not interfere with moving the saw.

The stops allow for setting the track quickly for 45° left- and right-hand miter cuts. Use an adjustable bevel to position the track at in-between points. You can add other pivot points for frequently used odd angles.

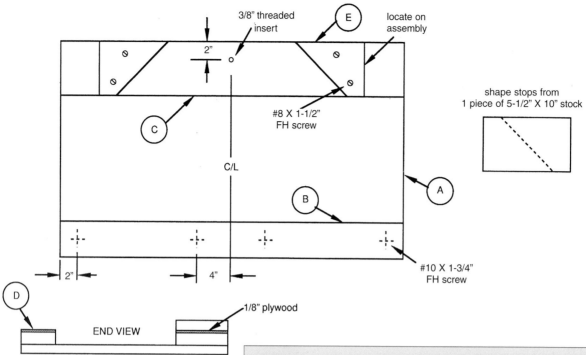

3/8" threaded insert

locate on assembly

shape stops from 1 piece of 5-1/2" X 10" stock

2"

E

C

C/L

#8 X 1-1/2" FH screw

A

B

2"   4"

#10 X 1-3/4" FH screw

D

1/8" plywood

END VIEW

Locate and drill the ⅜″ hole at one end of the track assembly.

STEP 3: INSTALL THE STOPS (REFER TO DRAWING ABOVE)

Prepare the stops by cutting them from a single piece of material. It's best to make the 45° cut on a scroll saw or band saw and then sand the sawed edges.

Put the track in place on the base by threading the ⅜″ × 1½″ bolt into the threaded insert in the rear fence. Rotate the track and use a combination square to mark its 45° right-hand position. Hold the track in place by tightening the bolt and using a clamp at the front fence. Install the right-hand stop by using glue and two no. 8 × 1½″ flathead screws.

Repeat the procedure to install the left-hand stop.

MATERIALS LIST

CROSSCUT AND MITER JIG

QTY.	KEY	NAME	SIZE (IN INCHES)	MATERIAL
1	A	Base	¾ × 24 × 40	Plywood
1	B	Fence	1½ × 3½ × 40	Pine or Fir
1	C	Fence	1½ × 5½ × 40	Pine or Fir
1	D	Crosscut Riser	⅛ × 3½ × 40	Plywood
1		Miter Riser	⅛ × 5½ × 40	Plywood
2	E	Stop (Both From 1 Piece)	¾ × 5½ × 10	Pine or Fir

Track

QTY.	KEY	NAME	SIZE (IN INCHES)	MATERIAL
2	F	Support	⅜ × 3½ × 44	Plywood
2	G	Arm	¾ × 3 × 32	Pine or Fir
2	H	End	¾ × 4 × 13½	Pine or Fir
2	I	Filler	⅜ × 4 × 6½	Plywood

No. 10 × 1¾″ Flathead Screw (8)

No. 8 × 1½″ Flathead Screw (4)

⅜″ Threaded Insert (1)

⅜″ × 1½″ Bolt with Fender Washer (1)

¼″ × 1⅝″ Steel Rod

Optional Bushings

QTY.	KEY	NAME	SIZE (IN INCHES)	MATERIAL

1⅛″ × ¼″ ID × ¾″ OD (3)   ½″ × ¼″ ID × ¾″ OD (3)

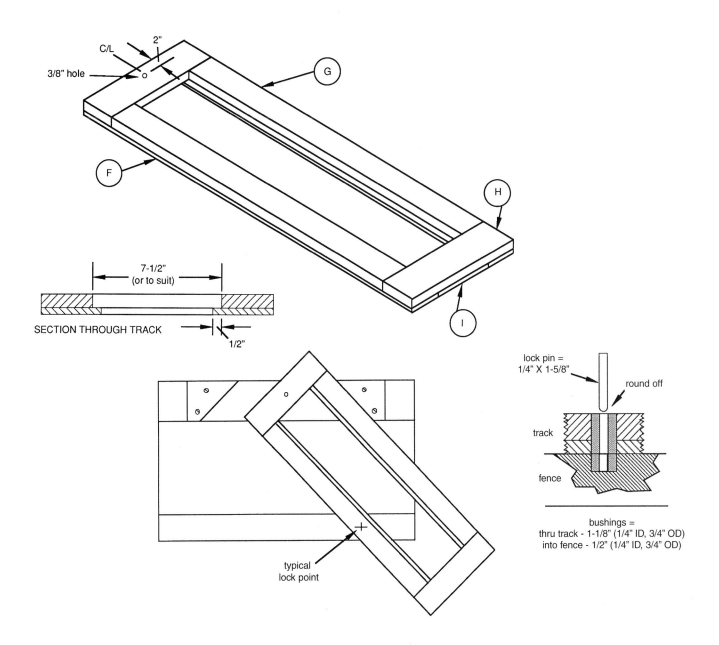

SECTION THROUGH TRACK

7-1/2"
(or to suit)

1/2"

C/L

2"

3/8" hole

typical
lock point

lock pin =
1/4" X 1-5/8"

round off

track

fence

bushings =
thru track - 1-1/8" (1/4" ID, 3/4" OD)
into fence - 1/2" (1/4" ID, 3/4" OD)

STEP 4: LOCATE THE LOCK POINTS

Swing the track to its 45° right-hand position and secure it with the bolt. Drill a ¼″ hole through the left arm of the track into the center of the front fence. Use a square to position the track for crosscutting and, again through the track's left arm, drill a ¼″ hole. Repeat the procedure with the track in its left-hand position. This time, the lock point will be in the track's right arm.

Since holes through wood can be abused by continual use, you can as-sure continued accuracy by taking the trouble to install bushings, at all lock points. Drill slightly undersize holes for the bushings and tap them into place after coating them with epoxy. If you plan to use bushings, drill ⅙″ pilot holes instead of ¼″ holes when you locate the lock points.

USING THE JIG

If you need to saw angles between 0° and 45°, set the track with an adjust-able bevel and secure it with a small clamp. If the odd angle is needed fre-quently, install an additional lock point.

You can form straight or angled dadoes by adjusting the blade's pro-jection for the depth of cut needed and making repeat passes. Make out-line cuts first to marks on the work, then clean out the waste between them.

Portable Drill Light-Duty Sanding Station

The split clamp arrangement should be made to grip the drill tightly. If you find the drill's position isn't stable enough, place a block of wood under it for additional support. Adjust the torque feature of the drill, if there is one, before installing.

The modern portable electric drill ranks as one of the more versatile power tools because of the myriad accessories available for it. Driving sanding drums and small abrasive discs are among its hand-held applications but, in this area, keeping the tool still while you apply the work is often a more convenient way to operate. In my case, it's because I often provide miniatures to preview the design and proportions of projects I plan to build. So I do sanding chores on the model components on a small, shop-made, drill-powered sanding station rather than on full-size sanding machines.

The sanding station isn't necessarily limited to that particular chore. Anyone whose interests include activities like making doll-house furniture, reproducing classic pieces in miniature size or constructing model boats, will find the project useful. Actually, once on hand, the sanding station proves useful for more "extreme" applications.

The drum sander's face provides support for the work and ensures that sanded edges will be square to adjacent surfaces. Use a drum with a diameter that closely matches the curve being sanded. Move the accessory frequently so the entire abrasive area of the drum can be utilized.

Position the disc sander unit about ⅛″ away from the disc's surface. If the drill has a reversing feature, workpieces can be placed on either the left or right side of the table. Remember that sanding is a "smoothing" job. It's not a good idea to rely on sanding to remove a large amount of material.

Always use the guard when doing chores like buffing—and always wear safety goggles. This setup can also be used with wire brushes, or even a small grinding wheel.

Use a tapered piece of wood to keep the drill's trigger depressed. The component will provide speed control, assuming the drill's trigger is a factor in that area.

MAKING THE JIG

STEP 1: PREPARE A BASE

Cut the base to the size shown in the materials list and mark it with a longitudinal centerline. Install the two ⁵⁄₁₆″ threaded inserts on the base's centerline so they are a bit below the part's surface. It isn't necessary to supply the guard at this time.

STEP 2: CONSTRUCT THE DRILL-MOUNT

Cut part (A) to size and draw a centerline along its length. Mark a second line to intersect with the centerline 4″ from what will be the mount's base. Using the intersection of the lines as a center, work with a fly cutter (or a hole saw if one of suitable diameter is available) to form a hole that

suits the area of the drill at the rear of the chuck. Be sure to clamp the mount and a backing board securely to the drill press table and feed the cutter slowly at minimum rpm.

Draw the profile of the top part of the mount and saw it to shape on a scroll saw or band saw. Drill pilot holes for the two 1½″ sheet metal screws. Then, prepare the mount as

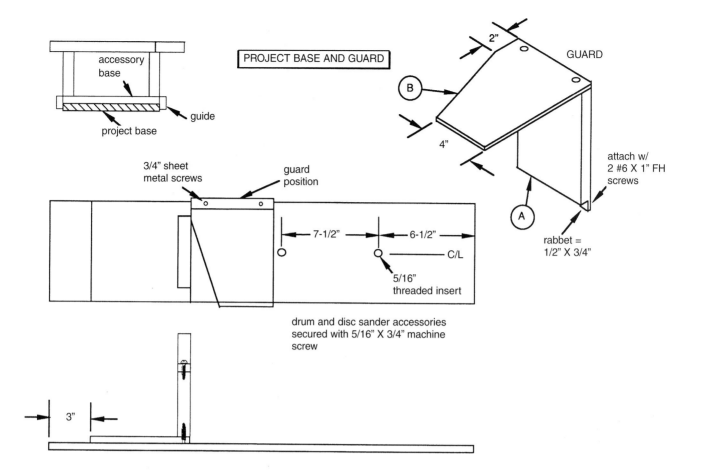

accessory base

project base

guide

2"

GUARD

B

4"

attach w/
2 #6 X 1" FH
screws

A

rabbet =
1/2" X 3/4"

3/4" sheet
metal screws

guard
position

7-1/2"

6-1/2"

C/L

5/16"
threaded insert

drum and disc sander accessories
secured with 5/16" X 3/4" machine
screw

3"

two pieces by sawing on the hole's horizontal centerline.

Cut the base of the drill-mount (B) to size and put the two components together with glue and three no. $10 \times 1\frac{1}{2}''$ flathead screws. Be certain that the angle between the base and the mount is 90°. Mark the location of the assembly on the project's base (C) and attach the assembly permanently by using glue and four no. $6 \times 1''$ flathead screws.

STEP 3: ASSEMBLE DRUM SANDER ACCESSORY

Start by sizing the part for the base (A). Form the $\frac{1}{4}'' \times 5''$ slot on the base's centerline by drilling a $\frac{1}{4}''$ end-hole and then sawing away the waste.

Prepare the guides (D) and attach them to the base with glue and 3d finishing nails. It's important for this assembly to slide smoothly on the project's base; so make a test and, if

MATERIALS LIST				
DRILL SANDING STATION				
Drill Mount				
QTY.	KEY	NAME	SIZE (IN INCHES)	MATERIAL
1	A	Mount	$\frac{3}{4} \times 5 \times 6\frac{1}{4}$	Hardwood
1	B	Base	$\frac{1}{2} \times 6\frac{1}{2} \times 7$	Plywood
1	C	Project Base	$\frac{1}{2} \times 7 \times 31\frac{1}{4}$	Plywood

$1\frac{1}{2}''$ Sheet Metal Screw (2)

No. $10 \times 1\frac{1}{2}''$ Flathead Screw (3)

No. $6 \times 1''$ Flathead Screw (4)

Drum Sander				
QTY.	KEY	NAME	SIZE (IN INCHES)	MATERIAL
1	A	Base	$\frac{1}{2} \times 7 \times 10$	Plywood
1	B	Face	$\frac{3}{4} \times 7 \times 9\frac{1}{2}$	Plywood
2	C	Support	$\frac{3}{4} \times 1\frac{1}{2} \times 6$	Plywood
2	D	Guide	$\frac{1}{2} \times \frac{3}{4} \times 10$	Pine

No. $10 \times 1\frac{1}{2}''$ Flathead Screw (3)

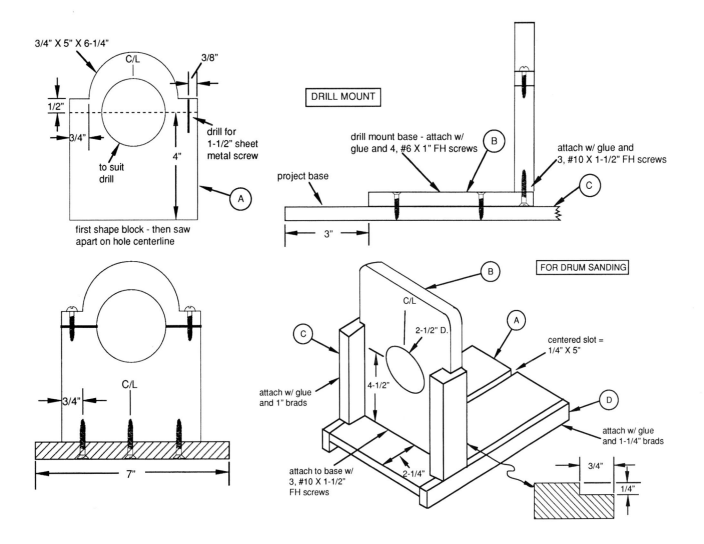

3/4" X 5" X 6-1/4"

C/L

3/8"

1/2"

3/4"

to suit drill

4"

drill for 1-1/2" sheet metal screw

A

first shape block - then saw apart on hole centerline

DRILL MOUNT

drill mount base - attach w/ glue and 4, #6 X 1" FH screws

B

attach w/ glue and 3, #10 X 1-1/2" FH screws

C

project base

3"

C/L

3/4"

C/L

7"

FOR DRUM SANDING

B

C/L

2-1/2" D.

A

centered slot = 1/4" X 5"

attach w/ glue and 1" brads

4-1/2"

C

attach to base w/ 3, #10 X 1-1/2" FH screws

2-1/4"

D

attach w/ glue and 1-1/4" brads

3/4"

1/4"

Disc Sander				
QTY.	KEY	NAME	SIZE (IN INCHES)	MATERIAL
1	A	Base	½ × 7 × 14	Plywood
2	B	Side	¾ × 3⅛ × 6½	Pine
1	C	Top	¾ × 8 × 10	Plywood
2	D	Guide	½ × ¾ × 14	Pine

No. 10 × 1½" Flathead Screw (8)

Project Base and Guard				
QTY.	KEY	NAME	SIZE (IN INCHES)	MATERIAL
1	A	Support	¾ × 6 × 8½	Plywood
1	B	Shield	⅛ × 6 × 7¾	Acrylic

⁵⁄₁₆" Threaded Insert (2)

No. 6 × 1" Flathead Screw (2)

¾" Sheet Metal Screw (2)

⁵⁄₁₆" × ¾" Machine Screw with Washer (1)

necessary, do some judicious sanding on the inside surfaces of the guides.

Prepare the part for the face (B) and mark it with a vertical centerline. Draw a horizontal line 4½" from what will be the part's bottom edge. Using the intersection of the lines as a center, use a fly cutter or hole saw on the drill press to form the 2½"-diameter hole.

Supply the supports (C) by starting with stock that is long enough for two parts. Form the ¼"-deep × ¾"-wide rabbet along one edge, and then saw the piece to obtain the parts that are needed. Attach the supports to the face with glue and 1" brads.

Mark the location of the face/support-assembly on the base and, after applying glue to contact areas, hold the two assemblies together with small bar clamps as you install the three no. 10 × 1½″ flathead screws.

STEP 4: MAKE THE DISC SANDER ACCESSORY

Start this phase of the project as you did the assembly for drum sanding. That is, prepare the base (A) and then attach the guides (D) with glue and 3d finishing nails. Next, cut the sides (B) to size and, after applying glue to mating areas, hold the sides in place with clamps while you install the no. 10 × 1½″ flathead screws.

Cut the top (C) to size. Form the L-shaped notch at the top's front edge on a scroll saw or band saw. Install the top with glue and four no. 10 × 1½″ flathead screws.

STEP 5: ADD THE GUARD

Saw the support (A shown on page 156) to size and then form a ½″-deep × ¾″-wide rabbet along its bottom edge. Attach the support to the project's base with two no. 6 × 1″ flathead screws. Do not use glue.

I used Lexan for the shield, but any rigid acrylic will do. Attach the shield to the support with two ¾″ sheet metal screws.

STEP 6: MAKE A SANDING DISC

Sanding discs for portable drills usually have a rubber backing, so they're not ideal for use with the sanding station. However, you can easily make one, as I did. Form a ¾″-thick × 6″ diameter disc. This can be done by working on the drill press with a fly cutter or by sawing on a scroll saw or band saw. If the latter method is used, sand the sawed edges smooth on a disc sander, preferably by using a pivot guide (see page 120).

Bore a blind centered hole in the disc to receive the ⅜″ threaded insert. Install the insert so it is a bit below

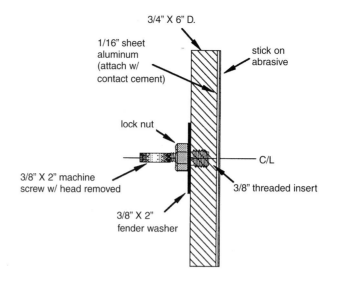

MAKE A DISC

3/4" X 6" D.

1/16" sheet aluminum (attach w/ contact cement)

stick on abrasive

lock nut

3/8" X 2" machine screw w/ head removed

C/L

3/8" threaded insert

3/8" X 2" fender washer

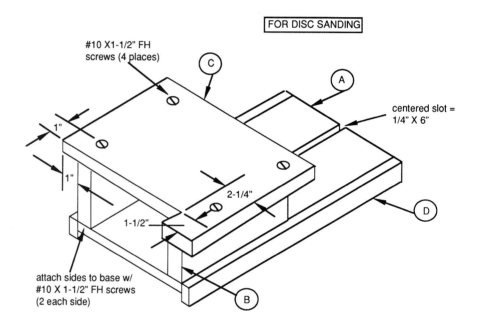

FOR DISC SANDING

#10 X1-1/2" FH screws (4 places)

C

A

centered slot = 1/4" X 6"

1"

1"

2-1/4"

1-1/2"

D

attach sides to base w/ #10 X 1-1/2" FH screws (2 each side)

B

the surface of the disc. Cut the aluminum cover just a bit oversize and, after attaching it to the disc with contact cement, sand it to conform to the perimeter of the disc. Use fine sandpaper or emery to "break" the sharp edge of the aluminum disc.

Remove the head from a ⅜″ × 2″ machine screw. Thread the lock nut onto the screw, add the fender washer and, after installing the screw so it bottoms in the insert, tighten the lock nut.

USING THE JIG

The drum sander and disc sander tables slide on the project's base. Apply paste wax or a dry lubricant to contact areas occasionally to keep the action smooth. Both of the units are secured to the base with the 5/16 × ¾″ machine screw. Position the disc sander table so it is about ⅛″ from the sanding disc's surface. Since most modern drills have a reversing feature, it's possible to use either side of the disc for sanding.

INDEX